Central New York Mountain Biking

The 30 Best Back Road & Trail Rides in Upstate New York

Dick Mansfield

Vitesse Press
4431 Lehigh Road, #288
College Park, Maryland 20740

Cover Photograph by Eric Sanford/MOUNTAIN STOCK

All other photographs by the author

Cover design by Bill Woodruff

Route maps by James P. Kuehl/Cogan Associates

Library of Congress Cataloging-in-Publication Data

Mansfield, Dick, 1940-
   Central New York mountain biking : the 30 best back road & trail rides in Upstate New York / Dick Mansfield
         p. cm.
   ISBN 0-937921-50-5 : $12.95
   1. All terrain cycling—New York (State) —Guidebooks. 2. Bicycle trails—New York (State) — Guidebooks. 3. New York (State) — Guidebooks. I. Title.
   GV1045.5.N7M36 1994
   797.6'4'09747—dc20   94-2715
                                       CIP

Printed in the United States of America

4   5   6   7   8   9   10

To Mary,
for her ongoing support and encouragement.

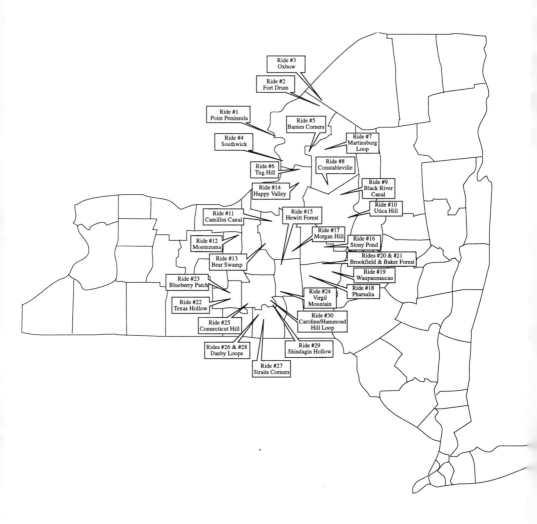

Table Of Contents

Introduction

Central New York is a mountain bike rider's dream. There is a wonderful variety of riding ranging from single-track trails through mud and ruts which will challenge the most serious of riders to smooth, shaded dirt roads that will be just right for those looking for a quiet jaunt away from traffic.

This book is designed for riders of all abilities. I selected the rides for this book based on my exploration and experience (having lived in the area for nearly twenty years.) Each ride is classified according to ease of riding into one of three categories: *Beginner, Intermediate*, or *Advanced*. Most rides have climbing early and in the middle, and then finish with a glide back to the starting point. Novices can take their time, push the bike up hills, and make a day of it. Hard-charging experts looking for a workout can strap on an extra water bottle and blast off — there are some tough rides described herein.

One of the features of Central New York is that it has dozens of state forests and wildlife management areas with miles of hiking and cross-country ski trails that are perfect for mountain bike riding. Many of the rides in this book incorporate these networks of off-road trails, often in conjunction with some back roads.

In the southern tier of the region, the Finger Lakes Trail (FLT), a trail network which connects the Allegheny Mountains with the Catskills and which has nearly 700 miles of hiking trails, runs through much of the area covered by this book. While some of the rides described in this book incorporate FLT segments, the use of parts of the trail by mountain bikes is under discussion. Observe any restricted signage and do your part, through responsible riding and trail stewardship, to keep the trail available for multiple uses.

A farmland vista on the Labrador Twin Loops circuit. (Ride 17)

Central New York is steeped in history. From the War of 1812 sites on Lake Ontario to the Native American campgrounds in the Southern Tier, these bike routes traverse a wide range of American history. Some of the trails you will try were likely first traveled by Native Americans. Others are old wagon roads that cross areas once farmed by early settlers. Much of the poor soil was abandoned during the Depression, but the vestiges of their early labors show through the underbrush and the trees. You'll pedal by old stone walls and cemeteries, crumbling cellar holes with ancient lilac trees blooming nearby, and gnarled apple trees whose fruit once provided jams and jellies for the hard-working families.

Although there are thousands of mountain bike owners in upstate New York, you'll have the trails to yourself. In the hours of riding the routes of this book, I met dozens of hikers, several equestrians, a group of llama trekkers, but only three mountain bikers.

Mountain Bike Etiquette

All the rides in this book are on public rights-of-way or public land. The only exceptions are several stretches of the Finger Lakes Trail where private landowners have given permission to use their land. Stay on the marked trails — it is critical to the future of mountain biking in New York that we ride responsibly.

Many of the lovely places we ride through are fragile, especially in the spring and fall wet seasons. We can wear out our welcome fast by leaving knobby-tired prints in May that will still be there in August. As much as I love mud, I try, whenever possible, to avoid leaving a lot of tire tracks and marking up the trail. So stay off environmentally-sensitive terrain such as wetlands, muddy soils on slopes, and soft hiking trails. Practice good outdoor ethics: carry out what you carry in, do not litter, camp in designated areas, and respect the privacy of others.

IMBA, the International Mountain Biking Association, is a group committed to educating the public in the safe and responsible use of mountain bicycles. They put it this way in their Rules of the Trail:

1. **RIDE ON OPEN TRAILS ONLY.**

2. **LEAVE NO TRACE.**

3. **CONTROL YOUR BICYCLE.**

4. **ALWAYS YIELD THE TRAIL.**

5. **NEVER SPOOK ANIMALS.**

6. **PLAN AHEAD.**

Moving On

Are these the best 30 mountain bike rides in Central New York? Why not add your favorites to the list? Talk to avid off-road riders; visit some of the excellent local bike shops and talk to their staff about riding suggestions. Read Fif*ty Hikes In Central New York* by Bill Ehling as well as the *Tug Hill Recreation Guide*. Check with the New York Department of Environmental Conservation in Cortland and Sherburne. Join the Finger Lakes Trail Conference and the Tug Hill Ski Club.

Use this book as a launching pad and you will find dozens of other trail and back road riding opportunities. If you want to share your "finds" with others, please send a brief description to: Vitesse Press, 4431 Lehigh Road, #288, College Park, MD 20740.

Watertown Area Rides

Point Peninsula Loop   28 miles
Beginner/Intermediate

Fort Drum   19.5 miles
Beginner -- Flat and mostly pavement

Oxbow Ride   22 miles
Intermediate

Southwick Beach Nature Tour   6 miles
Beginner -- Mostly trails

An historic church marks the start of the Oxbow Ride.

Point Peninsula Loop

28 Miles

Beginner/Intermediate

This is a flat picturesque tour of Point Peninsula on paved and dirt roads. The ride can be shortened to 16 miles by starting at the isthmus. This is a good ride to do early in the day before campers and tourists are up and about.

How To Get There

Take Exit 46 off Route 81 and follow Route 12E through Chaumont and Three Mile Bay toward Cape Vincent.

Watch for the turn for Point Peninsula about 1.8 miles west of Three Mile Bay. There is a convenience store which has a large parking lot. Ask for permission to park.

As mentioned above, if you want a shorter ride, you can continue driving toward Point Peninsula and park at the isthmus. This shortens the ride by twelve miles and avoids the heavier traffic along North Shore Road.

The Ride

As you leave Route 12E, there's a small cemetery nestled in the shade to your left just as you start climbing one of the only hills on this ride. You may want to explore that on the way home.

Be watchful for traffic during this first stretch. The road is gently rolling and at times has a lot of vacation traffic. There's a bike lane, but it is rough and quite narrow. After 1.5 miles, there's a lovely view of Chaumont Bay and several promontories. The small island you can see is called Cherry Island.

Take the well-marked turn to the left toward Long Point State Park at Mile 2.8. The riding continues to be smooth and easy as you pass many camps and camping grounds. You come right up to the

Old cemeteries reflect the history of the area.

water at Mile 5.7 where there's a marina and market. Round the bend and ride along the isthmus — perhaps stopping for a moment to watch the anglers or the waves washing up on the granite blocks along the roadway. (Here is where you can park if you want to shorten the ride by about 12 miles.)

At the end of the isthmus (Mile 6.2), take the left on pavement toward the state park. You'll again see a lot of summer camps along the water as well as some hay fields for local farmers. Continue past the paved road to the right at Mile 8.2 (Shore Road).

The entrance to the state park is at Mile 9.4. Long Point State Park (315-649-5258) offers camping and boating. Unless you want

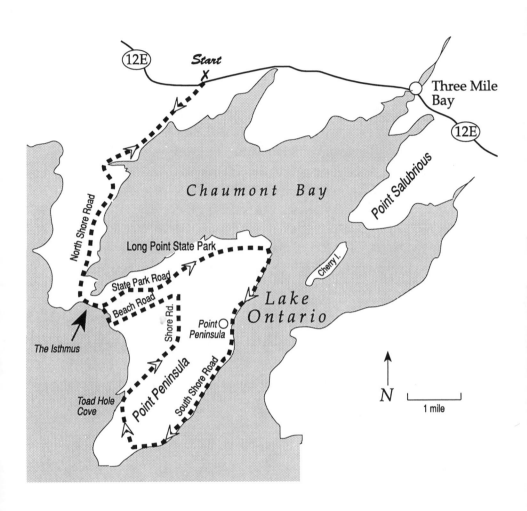

to check it out for a future excursion, pedal past and continue on to Clines Point at Mile 10.5. This is a sharp right turn that brings you right down to the water.

Pedal along the narrow road that follows the shoreline. There are many camps along through here — it's beautiful biking. The water is very inviting. You may wish to stop at an uninhabited spot and wade or swim.

Just a half mile ahead there's an intersection. Turn left toward the water and pick up South Shore Road. You'll be entering what is called the Village of Point Peninsula. Enjoy several miles of easy riding with lovely views off to the left across the water. The road is narrow and lightly traveled. At Mile 15.5, note the vacation homes with their very unusual street signs.

A half mile further, there's a right turn which will lead away from the water. Stay on the main road as you pass by swampy hay fields. A mile later, turn left (Mile 19.8) on to the dirt road (Beach Road).

This is a pretty stretch of dirt road through hay fields that will swing you back around to the isthmus at Mile 22.

Before you head the six miles back to Route 12E, you may want to stop for a cold drink at the marina. Be cautious with traffic on the way back and enjoy the last little descent down to the starting point.

Fort Drum

19.5 miles

Beginner — Flat and mostly pavement

Imagine the quiet of a back road ride suddenly punctuated by the shriek of a diving F-16 or the rumble of an Apache helicopter. If you like to watch military aircraft, this mountain bike ride may be your cup of tea. Pick a day with good weather — Fridays and Saturdays are often heavy flying days. If jets don't interest you, you might want to try some of the other rides outlined in the book.

The Fort Drum military reservation has a vast target complex that draws aircraft from as far away as Michigan. This bike route parallels the reservation and provides some excellent vantage points for observation. Most of the route is on pavement, but several of the roads are nearly impassable to vehicular traffic. This is an easy level ride that is well-suited for a family outing.

How To Get There

Take Route 81 north past Watertown to the Route 11 exit. From the intersection of Route 11 and Route 342, head north on Route 11 through Evans Mills and Philadelphia. As you approach Antwerp, you'll see a sign for "Military Aircraft Maneuvers." There is a parking/picnic area just ahead on the right. (14.8 miles from the Route 11/342 intersection.)

From the north, take Route 11 south from Gouverneur. Pass by the Village of Antwerp and watch for the parking area on your left about a mile out of town.

The Ride

Head north out of the parking area and turn right down Coolidge Road toward the Indian River. This is marked as a seasonal highway and you will soon see why. Pass under the ConRail bridge and there will be an old concrete bridge across the river to your right. That is where you will return at the end of the ride.

Staying on the Route 11 side of the river, bear to the left along the old asphalt road which parallels the railroad track and the highway. Note the old concrete guard rails — as you've guessed, this was once the "main drag" heading north. Passing by some abandoned farm fields in the first mile, you'll come to some interesting ledge outcroppings as you enter the wooded area. You also, as too often is the case on rural rides, pass by some illegal trash dump sites.

Isn't it nice to be riding a mountain bike over the dozens of rough spots and potholes on this beat up old road? Cruise down the nice downhill into the Village of Antwerp where you will come to an intersection at Mile 1.9. Turn left on Mechanic Street, cross the railroad track, and head toward Route 11.

Carefully cross Route 11 and turn left, heading south on the wide bike lane. You'll pedal for just several hundred yards before coming to a paved road that leads off to the right. Take it. This is a smooth country road but don't be complacent, drivers whip along and don't expect to see cyclists. Ride defensively. You may spot some brown and white cows along this road as well as several lovely weathered barns. The remaining groves of sugar maples are those that have escaped the ravages of road salt — so far.

If you enjoy geology, this is a ride that really points out the shallowness of the topsoil in upstate New York. Long ledges are exposed in the fields that you pass as you start an easy downhill to the intersection with Holkins Road at Mile 5.3. Continue straight.

You are now riding on Carpenter Road which is smooth and lightly traveled. At Mile 6.3, you'll come to Halls Corners. Cross straight ahead on the road marked "4 Ton Bridge" which is Keyes Road but which is unmarked.

At Mile 8, you'll come to the intersection with Ore Bed Road.

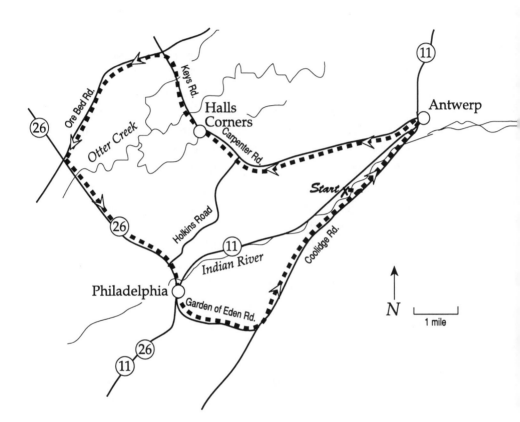

Turn left, staying alert for traffic as you enjoy the dips and climbs on your way to Route 26. It's not uncommon to see F-16 jets high to your left as they prepare to use the Fort Drum practice area.

You'll coast down to Route 26 at Mile 10.5. Turn left and head toward the Village of Philadelphia on the wide paved shoulder. It's an easy three mile cruise up to the intersection with Route 11.

As you approach Philadelphia, you will see the new water tank of the Village up ahead. This community is one of many in the area which changed dramatically in the late 1980's due to the major expansion at Fort Drum. As you near the village, cruise by Holkins Road coming in from the left. There is a convenience store at Route 11 if snacks or drinks are what sounds good about now.

To continue, turn right down Route 11, crossing the river and passing by the Indian River Central School until you come to Sand Street. (If you come to the overpass, you've ridden too far.) Sand Street will be on the left and passes initially through residential areas before bringing you to a railway crossing as you leave the Village. At the next intersection (Mile 14.8), you'll encounter the nicely-named "Garden of Eden" road which leads you east. Again, this is smooth with limited traffic. If there are any jets working the range, they will be flying up ahead.

At the intersection with Coolidge Road (Mile 16.2), turn left and head north. Coolidge Road, which has the military reservation just off to the right, will lead you back to the starting point. There are several farms and houses along this straight stretch and great vistas to the east for plane-watchers.

After two miles, you will come to a three-way intersection. Continue straight on to the unimproved road that will get a little rougher as you proceed. As you pedal down across the concrete bridge, things will look familiar. Make the sharp left turn, pedal under the railroad bridge, and climb up to the parking lot.

Oxbow Ride

22 miles

Intermediate

After a country ride on paved highways, you'll have some challenging riding on old wagon trails and farm roads, traveling through some desolate abandoned farm land. The return to Oxbow is on pavement. Make sure you bring some bug repellant; this is real deerfly and horsefly country!

How To Get There

From Route 11, the turn for Oxbow is a mile north of Antwerp and is marked with a sign from both the north and south. Take County Road 24 and follow the signs for six miles to the hamlet of Oxbow. There is parking along the main street beside the community green. A convenience store is right across the way for snacks and cold drinks. The rural nature of this town is reflected in the design of its post office, which you will definitely want to notice.

The Ride

Leave Oxbow and head west for a mile on the paved road past the road marked "Jefferson 25." After crossing two creeks, turn left toward Rossie at Mile 1.0 marked "St. Lawrence 30." This road has some traffic and not much of a shoulder, so ride carefully.

Pass by the first left turn at Mile 2 and start a gradual climb of about one half mile. Note the interesting cuts in the sandstone as you crest the hill. There's also an abandoned stone house to your left at Mile 3. Pedal past Scotch Settlement Road which comes in from right at Mile 4.4 and then enjoy the nice cruise down to the bridge over Indian River at Mile 5.0.

Just ahead on the left is Mine Road. Turn on to it and be alert, things could get interesting in a moment. You may have to deal with a farm dog or two so get your water bottle ready to spray. If they are out and barking, just pedal past them — once you are off their turf, they'll go home. At the farm, at Mile 5.4, take the "Seasonal Use Road" to the right. (River Road goes off to the left — you will be returning from that direction.)

This next stretch is some great mountain bike riding. The first climb is not only steep but technical with a lot of rough cobbles. Both sides of the road are fenced-off pasture with more trees than grass — typical upland pasture that dairy farmers have struggled with for more than a century.

As you climb at Mile 6.1, there are the remains of a stone house. Notice the ledge outcroppings through here — it's easy to see why the land is suited only for pasture — and even that is questionable due to the number of scrub trees.

After a quarter mile, you'll start a downhill on the farm road, which gets rougher as you go along. At Mile 7, just after you pass by several small hay fields still in active use, the road abruptly gets rougher and more overgrown with lots of grass in the middle. It results in several miles of great back country mountain bike riding.

Passing by several grown-over pastures, you'll see the old weather-beaten farmhouses that are now abandoned. From the terrain you've already noticed, you can get some understanding of how difficult it must have been to maintain a farm out here.

You'll have a half mile climb on rough road and then, at Mile 8.5, the road widens a bit as you pedal past a summer camp. Pass by another abandoned farm and at the intersection, bear left and ahead, through the trees, you'll spot several houses: Civilization! (That past stretch is great "off-the-beaten path" mountain biking.)

The riding will now be is relatively level, mostly dirt and rough-paved back roads. This is Grass Lake Road although it is not marked. You'll pass by a stable and at Mile 10.4, Hart Flats Road goes off to the left. Head that way on the pavement.

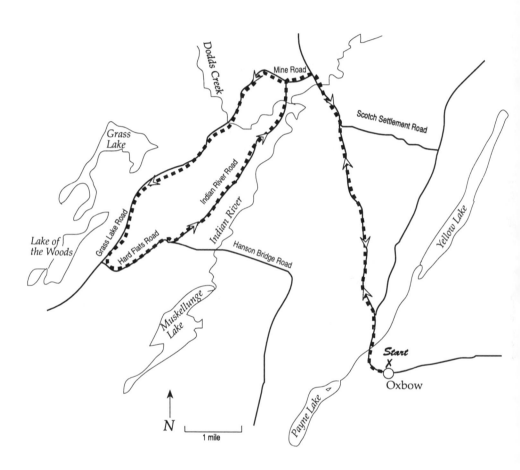

Dodds Creek

Mine Road

Scotch Settlement Road

Grass
Lake

Indian River Road

Indian River

Yellow Lake

Lake of
the Woods

Grass Lake Road

Hard Flats Road

Hanson Bridge Road

Muskellunge
Lake

Start
X
Oxbow

Payne Lake

N

1 mile

After a quarter mile, cruise down a nice little downhill watching out for the transition back to dirt at the bottom. This is an oiled-dirt surface road which is smooth and fast. You'll pass the Hanson Brook Road at Mile 11.7 but continue straight ahead on dirt. The road changes to pavement in another half mile. This is pretty farm country with little traffic. Coast down along the river and at Mile 15, you'll come to the "Canine Encounters" intersection with Mine Road. Bear right and retrace your route back out to the Rossie Road.

At Rossie, turn right across the river and climb back toward Oxbow. It is four miles back to the intersection with Jefferson County Road 25. (Mile 19.7)

Approaching Oxbow, you'll see Payne Lake off to the right. If you're up for more riding, read the note at the end of this description.) It is only one mile back to Oxbow from here.

Note

Interested in a diversion? Jefferson County 22 heads down to Payne Lake. This is a lovely little body of water with rugged cliffs on the far side. Be careful biking across the cattle guards in the road on the way to the state fishing access area.

Another option is Pulpit Rock, a large pothole in the face of cliff where, in 1820, the Reverend Oliver Leavitt preached to the pioneers. It is just 1/2 mile south of the hamlet on Pulpit Rock Road. There is a sign marking the site.

Southwick Beach Nature Tour

6 miles

Beginner — Mostly trails

Imagine a beach with fine light-colored sand, stretching as far as the eye can see. Where once a roller coaster dipped out over the small white-capped waves. Where fishing boats and yachts move across the far horizon. Cape Cod? The Bahamas? No, try Southwick Beach State Park, the starting point for a short easy ride that might well be combined with a day of picnics and swimming.

The route, suitable for beginning riders and virtually any kind of road bike, follows the two nature and fitness trails that have developed by the park. There is a short stretch along Route 3 but there is a wide bike lane.

How To Get There

Southwick Beach State Park (315-846-5338) is located off Route 3 on the shore of Lake Ontario. The 500 acre park has camping facilities and extensive picnic and bathing areas. It is easily reached from Route 81 by taking the Ellisburg exit and following Route 193 west until you come to the intersection with Route 3. There is a nominal admission fee during the summer.

The Ride

Pedal out of the parking area toward the park office. Just ahead on the right will be a cross-country ski trail logo and an illustrated map of the Dune Trail. You will be traversing a nature trail during the first mile, so be alert for hikers. The trail is easy riding, winding through wooded areas with just enough muddy patches, turns, and exposed roots to keep you alert. You'll encounter several wooden bridges and may have to hop the front wheel up on to them but they are wide and smooth.

After a half mile of winding trail, you'll pass by a trail that goes off to the left, back to the access road. The nature trail opens up into a pretty meadow filled with wildflowers and goldenrod. Keep straight ahead, cross Filmore Brook (which may well be dry), and enjoy the easy riding. At Mile 1, a wider road comes in from the left. Bear to the right and pedal down toward the wooden bridge, being watchful for soft sand. Note the extensive Southwick Marsh on your right.

A wooden foot bridge overlooks Southwick Marsh

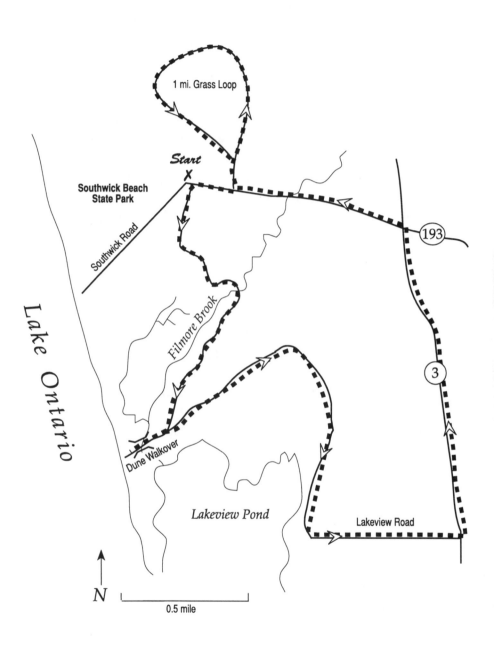

1 mi. Grass Loop

Start
X

**Southwick Beach
State Park**

Southwick Road

Filmore Brook

193

3

Dune Walkover

Lakeview Pond

Lakeview Road

Lake Ontario

N

0.5 mile

There's a barrier on the bridge so you should dismount and walk the bike. This will be a little side trip to take a look at the only fresh water dune system in New York state. The wooden walkover was constructed to protect this unique area from foot and bike traffic. If it is windy, notice how the dunes protect the marsh area — as you get closer to the lake, the wind will likely be much more noticeable.

When you are ready to proceed, reverse course and head back up the grass road. Pass by the trail you just came in on and cruise along on some easy jeep trail riding. There are a few rough spots to navigate as you pedal through overgrown farm fields now studded with sumac and other scrub trees. After a half mile, you'll see the silos and farm buildings along Route 3. The road swings to the south and at Mile 2.2, comes to a state boat launch on Lakeview Pond. Your route takes you to the left, out the dirt access road. You will hit Route 3 at Mile 2.7.

Cross Route 3 and turn left, heading back along the wide right shoulder for a mile. That's where you'll meet the intersection of Route 193 so turn left into the park and enjoy the nice smooth riding. You may want to ride on the smooth grassy area that lines the road. Pass by the cross country skier sign on the right and continue into the park. As you approach the entrance booth, watch carefully for a mowed trail off to the right. The park keeps it trimmed and it is like riding on a golf course green. You are hidden in the woods and will find this very enjoyable riding. This is a great one mile loop that will tempt you to "do a few laps." There are two exits — the one you entered and one that goes to the campground area. It's a quick spin back to the parking lot and the picnic and swim that should await you.

Extra Credit: Since this is such a short ride, you may want to do more riding. One moderately easy ride on pavement is to go out the access road, cross Route 3, and head out on Route 193. This is rolling farm land with several challenging hills. You can go out ten miles or more and then head back — resulting in a nice pedal through pretty Central New York countryside.

Tug Hill Area Rides

Barnes Corners Trail Ride   11.5 miles
Intermediate/Advanced -- Mostly trails

Tug Hill "Try-It"   11 miles
Intermediate/Advanced -- Single-track and dirt roads

Martinsburg Loop   24 miles
Intermediate -- Mostly dirt roads

Constableville Cruise   24 miles
Intermediate

"Times Square" marks the intersection of four trails. (Barnes Corners)

Barnes Corners Trail Ride

11.5 miles

Intermediate/Advanced — Mostly trails

Plan to get your bike a little muddy on this ride. Barnes Corners is famous in New York for the amount of snowfall it gets — and, as you will find, there's lots of water around year-round. This ride links up two public forests, the Tug Hill Forest and the Jefferson County Forest, each of which is blazed with a network of cross country ski trails. You will encounter some challenging mountain bike terrain. There are several steep climbs and many wet spots and creek crossings. There is also an option to do only the first loop of 3.8 miles.

How To Get There

The large parking area for the Tug Hill Forest is located on NY Route 177. From the east, take the Adams Center exit off Route 81 and head east on Route 177 for ten miles. The parking area is on the left (north) just a little over a half mile past the Route 178 intersection.

From Lowville, climb up towards Barnes Corners on Route 177. It is seventeen miles to the hamlet of Barnes Corners and a mile and a half more to the parking area. Barnes Corners has a small store if you need to stock up on munchies before or after the ride.

The Ride

Before you get started, let's talk a little about the trail system. Most of the trail for this ride is set aside for non-motorized use, so it tends to be rough and at times, unkempt. The Black River Chapter of the Adirondack Mountain Club maintains many of the trails so you will encounter a good number of stretches of corduroy road across the wet spots. Be prepared for some tricky bike riding — the log sections present a nice challenge. (Gear down, keep the weight off the front wheel, and give them a try.)

One of the many foot bridges. Jump your
front wheel over the logs and it's easy riding.

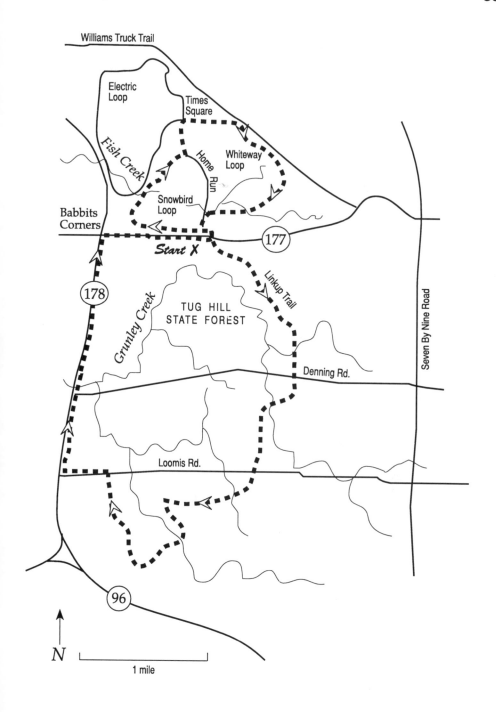

The ride starts off with a difficult section called the Snowbird Loop. Sign in at the trailhead and head out to the west on the loop. The first half mile will parallel Route 177 and you'll undoubtedly hear traffic off to your left. Immediately, you'll encounter your first few corduroy sections, a foretaste of some of the technical riding ahead. If they are too difficult, hop off and walk them — they're short. After a brief steep climb, enjoy the nice long gentle downhill as the trail swings away from the highway.

As you approach Fish Creek, there's a steep drop and then an equally steep, "get off and push", climb. The next half mile is a challenging stretch, especially if it is wet. Steep climbs, swampy areas, and corduroy sections will get you and your bike a little muddy. The intersection with Home Run Trail comes at Mile 1.5 but, due to the slow going, it may seem longer. Turn left and coast down the hard-packed road and navigate a long log road section as you come to the intersection called Times Square. (Mile 2.0)

As you can see from the signs on the trees, several trails begin here. The Electric Loop, so-named from the power lines, is 2.2 miles long. The John Young Trail is 1.7 miles long.

Turn sharply right on to the Whiteway Loop which will bring you back around to the starting point. This will be easier riding even though you still will have some swampy sections to negotiate. The trail climbs steadily and at Mile 2.6, passes the end of the John Young Trail.

Now comes a beautiful stretch of easy downhill riding through lovely well-trimmed pine trees. As you near the starting point, there'll be a couple more good short climbs, a screaming downhill, and you'll soon be out on the Homerun Trail. Turn left and head up to the starting point. (Mile 3.8)

Turn left and at the green storage shed, take a left onto the Linkup Trail that will head east and immediately cross Route 177. After cruising through a field of goldenrod, you'll be faced with your first steep climb as you pass through a grove of tamaracks.

These are definitely "hop off and push the bike" hills, especially the second one which is longer. Once you get on top, it's interesting riding through mixed hardwoods. Some parts are easy, some very technical with ruts and rocks, and every so often, a stream crossing. The wooden bridges offer you a chance to bunny hop up on to them. At Mile 5.3, coast down to Denning Road. Cross it and continue straight ahead, following the yellow D.E.C. disks on the trees.

Cruising through a pine grove on the Whiteway Loop.

The first stretch of this section is easy riding, however, about now, you may wish that the AMC members were a little less generous with their corduroy trail improvements. Often it is easier to splash through a mucky puddle than to jounce your way over log sections. (However, the improvements are welcomed by cross country skiers and hikers.) There's a nice descent down to the bridge over Grunley Creek (Mile 6) and after you climb up the opposite bank, the riding gets a bit more difficult with a few more roots and rough spots until you get to Loomis Road.

As you cross Loomis, look down the bank. If it is summertime, you're likely to view a green gooey waterhole. You'll be challenged to navigate through or around the swampy quagmire but, as soon as you scramble up the bank on the other side, you'll come to a much more sane creek crossing with a wooden bridge. At Mile 7, the trail arrives at the intersection with the Jefferson County Forest trail system.

These are multiple use trails and tend to be wider and smoother. By turning left, there is a nice loop here if you want to add distance but since this has been a pretty good workout, go ahead and turn right and head west. You will pass a trail to the right — keep straight ahead. In about a half mile of easy riding, you'll come to a "T" intersection. Turn right and pedal the easy .8 miles back up to Loomis Road.

At Loomis, turn left and head west on the dirt. It is three-quarters of a mile out to Route 189. Turn right at the pavement and you'll be looking at a quarter-mile climb to the top of the ridge. As you crest the rise, you'll see the Tug Hill Forest up ahead.

There's usually not much traffic on Route 189 but there is also no shoulder so be alert as you enjoy the smooth riding. At Mile 10.7, you'll come to Route 177. Turn right and travel up the wide bike lane — the parking area is less than a mile up the road on the right.

Tug Hill "Try-It"

11 miles

Intermediate/Advanced — Single-track and dirt roads

Be prepared for some wet spots and mud on this ride which follows much of the route of the famous Tug Hill 17K cross country ski race. It mixes some steep climbs with quite a few boggy areas and creek crossings. The last portion of the ride is on truck trails and dirt roads. If you want a longer ride, there are many ways to extend the ride using the Tug Hill Tourathon Trail network. See the Tug Hill Recreation Guide for more information.

How To Get There

The large parking area for the Tug Hill Tourathon is located at the intersection of Center and Wart Roads in the Town of Boylston. Take the Sandy Creek/Lacona exit off Route 81 and turn east to go through Lacona to the Lacona-Orwell road. Turn north at the intersection and in less than a mile, turn right on Center Road. (The turns are marked with "skier" signs.) The parking area is 3.0 miles down Center Road. Turn left at the stop sign.

The Ride

From the parking area, head north on Wart Road and just after the first rise, watch for the trail off to the right marked "Winona Way." Head into the woods and you will start a gentle climb for the next half mile. The riding will be muddy in spots and will parallel some old stone walls from long-gone farms. If there are ruts from

Tug Hill Tourathon Trails provide over 30 miles of dirt road and trail riding.

four-wheel drives, try to ride in the center —the trail will be drier as you climb. There is one good downhill followed, after some easy riding, by a fairly steep climb. You may spot a brook, Little Sandy Creek, off to the right through the trees. At Mile 1.7, you will come to the Hawley Truck trail. Turn right and climb up to the four-way junction at Mile 2.0.

Continue straight ahead, across Bargy Road on to Tucker Road

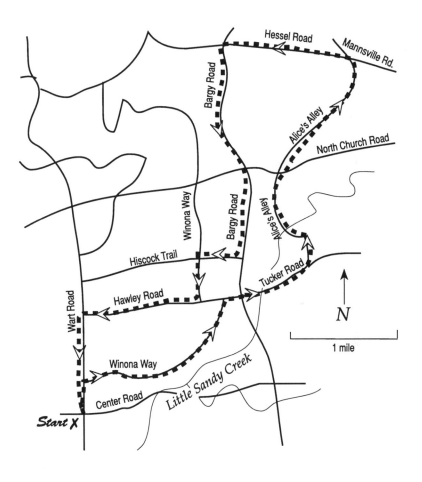

which will immediately pitch down into a nice descent. Let the bike run, there are no surprises at the bottom. You'll coast over two little streams and then be faced with a good climb. Gear down and crunch up the hill — it is about a quarter mile in length. Up on top, enjoy the easy riding on the smooth sandy road and start looking for the left turn on to "Alice's Alley," a ski trail, at Mile 3.0.

Alice's Alley is a favorite of many cross country skiers.

Alice's Alley is a favorite of many cross country skiers. It is challenging mountain biking, in other words — it's wet and has some downhills and uphills that test your riding ability. The downhills are all quite bumpy so plan to use your legs as shock absorbers.

The trail starts with some easy weaving through the hardwoods and then pitches down to cross Little Sandy Creek. (Watch for the wet spot at the bottom.) After crossing on the smooth wooden bridge, you may have to push your bike up the opposite bank — it often is quite wet. Heading into the pines, the riding is smooth but there is usually lots of standing water so plan to blast through some boggy areas. You probably will have wet feet and a mud streak up your back by the time you finish the descent down to the crossing of North Church Road at Mile 4.

The second half of Alice's Alley is easier riding. Cross North Church and climb up through the pines on the ski trail. Ignore the trail that bears to the right — always follow the yellow D.E.C. medallions. You'll enter a lovely hardwood forest as the trail levels and then have a long bumpy downhill through the woods which ends at a culvert and corduroy road stream crossing. (As you cruise along, you might visualize 500 ski racers following this same trail during the Tug Hill Tourathon.) There's one more rock-filled swampy section to negotiate before you follow an old farm road for the last few hundred yards up to the intersection at Mile 5.2 with the paved Mannsville Road and Hessel Road (dirt).

Swing sharply left on to Hessel Road. The first part of this road is level and fairly easy going. Ignore the private road going off to the left and get ready for some water-filled ruts and low spots. The base of this road is solid so you should be able to ride through most of the water without trouble. The last half mile down to the inter-section with Bargy Road is a steady downgrade. Turn left on Bargy.

Bargy Road will look like a thruway to you — smooth and sandy, it climbs gently through pines and hardwoods up to North Church Road at Mile 7.3. Cross and continue straight ahead. Note that there still are private camps in this area — you will pass one as you pedal south. Shortly after passing the camp, turn right on to the Hiscock Trail at Mile 8.0 and get ready for a mile and a half of fun — if wet, rocky riding is fun to you.

Just as you start on Hiscock you will come to a fork. Keep to the right, following the yellow discs. (Some of this route is marked with plain yellow medallions on the trees.) After dropping down a rocky descent, follow the markers through a logged-over area and a swampy creek crossing. There are many soft spots on this trail and you may find yourself doing some pushing. After little more than a half mile of fairly difficult going, Hiscock meets Winona Way. Take a sharp left on Winona.

Winona is rocky and has some soft spots as well but is fairly level. When you get to Hawley Road, turn right and enjoy the mostly downhill cruise on smooth dirt for about a mile. Just after Mile 10, you'll come upon Wart Road so turn left, cruise down the little hill and start climbing. You'll have a nice downhill, one more climb, and a last easy descent back down to the parking lot.

Martinsburg Loop

24 miles

Intermediate — Mostly dirt roads

The eastern edge of the Tug Hill plateau, rising abruptly from the level farmland, is eye-catching as you travel Route 26 and Route 12. This ride gives you a chance to climb up on to the plateau, explore some of the narrow dirt roads of the area, pause for a look at some of the natural wonders of the area, and finish with some easy cruising through Lewis County farmland. You can also, as an option, add some single-track riding on the Lewis County State Forest ski trails.

How To Get There
The ride starts in the middle of the hamlet of Martinsburg on Route 26. From Lowville, head south on Route 26 for four miles. From the south, take Route 12D out of Boonville and follow it north nine miles to Route 26. Continue north on Route 26 ten miles to Martinsburg. You can park near the library or on Route 26 in front of the Greystone Manor.

The Ride
Head south on Route 26 and right away, just as you start downhill, swing right on the paved Cemetery Street. Cruise out of the Village, past the large cemetery, and head out into farm country. At the intersection at Mile 1.3, cross West Road and climb straight ahead on Keener Hill Road.

You've got a half mile steady climb on loose gravel. Then, after a level stretch of a quarter mile, you will be climbing again through upland pastures. As you reach the top at Mile 2.3, pause to catch your breath and look back at the view. You've climbed about 700 feet in elevation. The good news is that the next twenty miles is mostly level riding. You're going to love riding these roads. They are smooth and sandy and just pleasant for pedaling — and there's hardly anyone around!

The road comes to an intersection at Mile 2.9. Continue straight ahead on the dirt/cinder road marked "Seasonal Use Highway." After a nice little cruise down across a small brook, there's a short climb up to a sharp left turn which is marked with a "10 MPH" road sign. As I huffed up by it, I found it amusing. No problem, Officer!

Veer left at the next junction at Mile 4.3 (You have probably already guessed from some of the signs, that these roads are part of the snowmobile network in the winter.) At Mile 5.2, turn left at the intersection, following the sign toward the Timber View Lodge.

"Seasonal Limited Use Highway" -- a mountain biker's welcome sign.

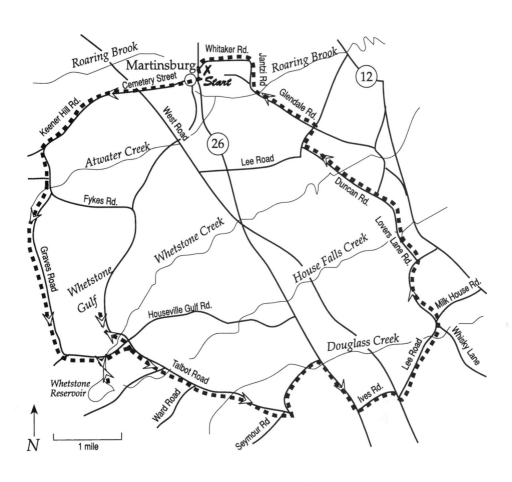

The route continues level, passing several roads. Stay on the main dirt road and at Mile 7.9, pass by an old farmhouse and continue ahead at the next "Seasonal Use Highway" sign.

At the next junction, Graves Corners (Mile 7.9), swing left. After pedalling less than a half mile, take the access road to the right into the Whetstone Reservoir. This is a nice place to stop and rest for a bit. There is a good chance you'll see some herons or ducks.

When you come back out from the reservoir, turn right, cross the creek, and go past the next turn (Talbot Road) and take the following left. Pedal down about a half mile and check out the Whetstone Gorge — it's well-marked with signs. Try the South Run trail — push your bike a few hundred yards down the trail and then leave it to check out the gorge on foot. It's spectacular.

Whetstone Gulf is two miles long and in spots, the nearly-vertical walls rise 350 feet. It is named for a grade of local sandstone that was once used on local farms as a whetstone. You may be able to spot it high up on the gorge walls — it will be light bands woven through the darker shale.

When you're through checking out the gorge, walk back up the trail and bike back to the intersection. Bear right and then immediately turn left on to Talbot Road. At Mile 10, you'll start a gentle downhill run passing by two roads coming in from the right. Cruise straight ahead on the wide cinder road.

You will pass by Ward Road and shortly afterwards, the Carpenter Cemetery at Mile 12.2. This is a nice easy downgrade on dirt. At Mile 13, you'll start down more seriously and have some wonderful views off to the left.

Want some trail riding? Right after Timber View Lodge, you can turn right and climb up Seymour Road to link up with the Lewis County Ski Trails at the State Forest. There are several loops, all marked with D.E.C. medallions. It's great single-track riding.

Just down the hill past the State Forest there's a sharp left turn. It's now a steady descent so let the bike run. Before you know it, you're back to Route 26, at Mile 14.4.

Turn right and head south on the shoulder of Route 26. You've got about a mile to ride before you will see Ives Road on the left.

GORGE TRAIL
> DANGEROUS <
PROCEED AT YOUR OWN RISK.
STAY ON MAIN TRAIL.
KEEP AWAY FROM CLIFF EDGES.
BEWARE OF FALLING ROCKS &
LOOSE STONES ON TRAIL.

Whetstone Gulf is a popular geological attraction.

Ives Road cuts through farm fields. At the first intersection, turn right toward the large farm and then take an immediate left turn on to the paved road at Mile 16.5. This is Lee Road which has a number of dairy farms. At Mile 17.3, you'll coast down a little drop — and cruise by Whiskey Lane and Milk House Road. (The folks who named roads around here outdid themselves — the next turn will be Lover's Lane Road.)

So, just as you get started down at Mile 16.5, turn left on to the dirt Lover's Lane Road. You can see Route 12 off to the east. Pedal over the new bridge at House Falls and continue on the level dirt road. There's an easy climb through a grove of shady maples as you approach the intersection at Mile 20. Continue straight ahead on the paved Duncan Road.

If you look off to the left, you'll spot the ridge where you were riding, up on the plateau, not long ago. The road goes to dirt as you pedal past a sugarhouse. See if you can spot some of the pipeline that brings the sap down from the maple groves.

At Mile 21.5, turn right and then take a left on Glendale Road. You can see Martinsburg up ahead. That blue silo is the community water tank.

As you pass the village park, take the dirt Jantzi Road which will bring you to up to Whitaker Road. Turn left and after one last steep climb, you'll be back at Route 26.

Constableville Cruise

24 miles

Intermediate

This ride climbs up the eastern edge of the Tug Hill Plateau, exploring a network of dirt roads and trails. Once the initial climb is over, you'll find easy riding up on the plateau because the terrain is level. Then there are several rocky trail sections to navigate and a great downhill run on a rough dirt road.

You will traverse an area that is wild — I saw a coyote during one ride, as well as several deer and red-tailed hawks. Much of the ride is through state forest lands.

How To Get There

The ride starts in the Village of Constableville, which is 25 miles north of Rome on Route 26. Take Route 12D out of Boonville to Potters Corners, then Route 26 to Martinsburg. If you come from the north through Lowville, take Route 26 south for four miles.

Constableville has a little village green, complete with band stand, at the northern edge of Main Street. Park there. A marker shows that this is the site of the first log cabin in Constableville, built in 1796. There is a "quick-stop" store with a snack bar just north of the village on Route 26. Why not take one of their apple turnovers with you to eat along the way?

The Ride

Head south on Main Street (toward the volunteer fire station) and turn right past the old hotel, heading up the paved (unmarked) High Market Road. This road goes to the hamlet of High Market, a favorite winter haven of area snowmobilers.

Climb up past the school and continue climbing on smooth pavement for a half mile. As the road levels some, note the lovely farmland on your right. At Mile 2.0, pedal by the turn for West Leyden and keep up the gradual climb — you've got about a mile to get to the top of the plateau. Isn't this fun?

At Mile 3.5, you're on the plateau and the road levels. Notice how the evergreens punctuate the skyline at this elevation. At Mile 4.6, turn right on the dirt road marked MacKay Road.

After a gentle climb through farm fields, the riding gets easier as you enter the hardwood forest. This is nice shady mountain biking through desolate country — here is where the coy-dog crossed the road in front of me — a sight which tends to get your attention. At Mile 6.0, you'll come to a four-corner intersection. Turn left on to Higby Road.

Higby is smooth and narrow, cutting across Sucker Brook at Mile 6.5. Can you spot the beaver dam down off to the left? A quarter mile later, the road gets rougher and as you enter the State Forest, the riding gets a little technical. The wheel ruts are rocky so you may want to stay on the grassy middle section. Once the riding smooths out, you will notice vestiges of old stone walls and apple trees — sure markers of old farmsteads now wild and overgrown. At Mile 7.5 at the dirt road intersection (North Road), turn right.

Head north on North Road through beeches and maples in the State Forest. At Mile 8.0, a dirt road comes in from the right — continue straight. You'll like the smooth riding along this stretch. At Mile 8.8, coast down to a "Y" with a road marked "Truck Trail" bearing left. Take the right fork.

You'll have some some nice gravel road riding for a few miles through the State Forest. At Mile 12, the Gomer Hill Road goes off to the right. Continue straight ahead.

At Mile 13.7, the ride comes to an intersection with Talbot Road

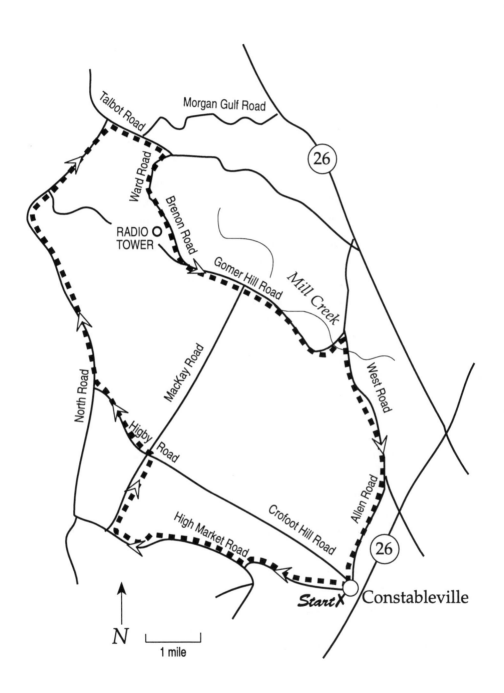

Talbot Road

Morgan Gulf Road

26

Ward Road

Brenon Road

RADIO O
TOWER

Gomer Hill Road

Mill Creek

North Road

MacKay Road

West Road

Higby Road

High Market Road

Crofoot Hill Road

Allen Road

26

Start ✗ Constableville

N

1 mile

and a gated forest road. Turn right. (The Martinsburg ride comes through some of this stretch.) You've got several miles of easy riding on wide cinder and dirt roads ahead. Cruise by Morgan Gulf Road which will be on your left at Mile 14.4 and get ready, as you come upon some open hay fields, to turn right at Mile 14.7 on the unmarked Ward Road.

At Mile 15.5, you'll come to a stop sign. Turn left and note the handsome weather beaten barn. You'll soon be coming out of the State Forest — a distinction made obvious by the vacation homes and "Land for Sale" signs. About Mile 16.3, if you look up to the right, you can see the FAA tower and lookout towers on Gomer Hill. (As a diversion, you might consider taking the half mile detour up to check the view out from the observation tower.) There are also some spectacular views from your bike off toward the Adirondacks as you approach the intersection with Gomer Hill Road.

The ride continues left down Gomer Hill on rough dirt road. After a mile, just after you pass a dairy farm, you'll pass MacKay Road on on the right — a road you've already been on earlier.

At Mile 18.7, turn left on the road marked "Seasonal Limited Use Highway." This turn comes up fast, so watch for it.

Now you've got a great two mile downgrade. As you start down, you can see, over the bank, one of the many gulfs that come off of Tug Hill. Keep your weight over the rear wheel, let your bike go and enjoy the steep winding descent. There are some rough gravel spots and a narrow one-lane bridge (which can provide a pretty good hop off the far end if you have the speed and nerve.) The road continues down the brook and comes out at Mile 20.5 on West Road. Turn right.

From here back to your starting point, it is easy riding on good pavement. Be careful, there's not much of a shoulder. Turn right on Allen Road at Mile 22.5. There's a brief climb of less than a half mile and then you'll see the village ahead. Coast down and at Mile 24, you're back at the starting point.

Utica Area Rides

Black River Canal Towpath   15 miles
Beginner

Utica Hill Climb   28 miles
Intermediate/Advanced -- Mostly pavement

Checking out one of the locks along
the Black River Canal Towpath.

Black River Canal Towpath

15 miles

Beginner

Back before the Erie Canal was even finished, Governor DeWitt Clinton began looking for more water to keep his "ditch" filled. He recommended tapping the Black River and after years of surveys and hassles, construction began in 1836. The canal began carrying water to Rome in 1849 and was opened to boat traffic in the next year. It served as the major link for moving lumber and other goods for 75 years until it was abandoned in 1922. Driving north to Boonville on Route 46 you can see vestiges of the old canal. More locks can be seen heading north from Boonville on Route 12 toward Lyons Falls.

A local group, with help from the state and communities, has established a trail along the old towpath from Boonville south. Closed to motorized vehicles, the trail is groomed for cross country skiing in the winter and used by hikers in the summer. It is a great mountain bike ride for the whole family since it is smooth riding with very little climbing. This is an out and back trip.

How To Get There
From Rome, take Route 46 north for 17 miles. The parking area is on the right 4.5 miles past the hamlet of North Western, just after you pass the Town of Ava sign. It is marked with a sign.

From Boonville, take Route 46 south past the Pixley Falls State Park. The parking area is on the left just after the Town Of Ava sign.

The towpath rises as you approach each lock.

The Ride

The trail heads north, parallel to Route 46. While the serenity of the setting may be broken by traffic noise from the highway, you'll enjoy some lovely views of the Lansing Kill River on the right as you pedal along. Just after a nice dip in the path and a short climb, cross the wooden bridge and climb up past the five combine locks. (This once was famous as the world's largest number of canal locks.). Plan to check them out on the return trip.

The towpath is smooth and level with short climbs each time you come to a lock. Many of the locks are covered with brush and trees but it's easy to spot where they are located — because you will come to another brief rise in the tow path. (The canal had 109 locks over its 35 mile length.)

At Mile 1.5, approaching Pixley Falls State Park, you will see the signs delineating State Park land. The small park has about 15 campsites, most of which you can see from the trail.

As the trail continues north, you will come to another wooden bridge complete with a waterfall at Mile 4. This section has water

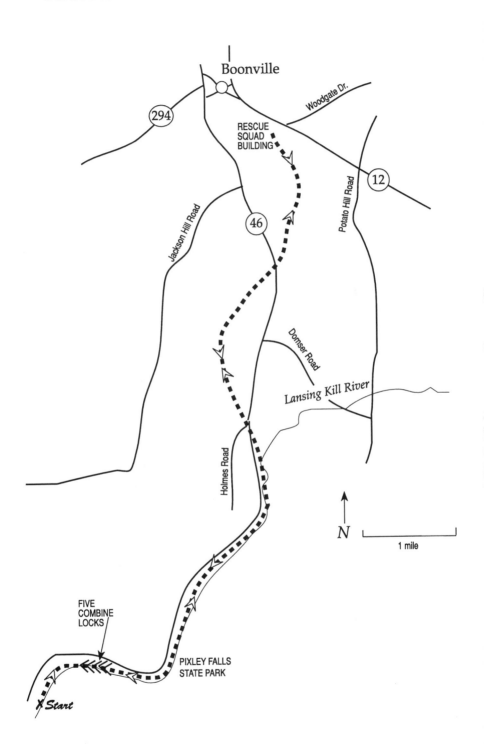

running through several of the old locks. The towpath crosses Route 46 just ahead at Mile 4.3.

Cross the highway carefully and cruise up the level farm path with the placid canal on your left. This loop will bring you back to Route 46 just before Mile 6. On the left at Mile 5.3, there is a footbridge going over the canal leading to cross country ski trails up the hill. This is an extensive ski network that invites further exploration. The trails, like the towpath, are maintained by BREIA, the Black River Environmental Improvement Association.

The towpath trail is maintained by BREIA, a local volunteer group.

After the second crossing of Route 46, you'll see an old stream gauging station up ahead and the path will become even more level. Much of the base is ledge so the riding is fast all the way to the trail's end (or beginning for those who might start in Boonville) at the Rescue Squad Building just off Route 12 in Boonville.

Retracing the route gives you some nice downhill runs as you pass each lock. Why not stop and explore several including the five lock combine near the trail's finish?

Utica Hill Climb

28 miles

Intermediate/Advanced — Mostly pavement

The area north of Utica is not only rich in history, it also is rich in winding back roads that, while paved, provide some interesting riding and real vertical challenges for mountain bikers. This route features some difficult climbs and descents during the first half and then some easier country riding for the rest of the route. It traverses rural areas that, because of their proximity to Utica, are becoming built up. It is easy to see, when you look off on some of the views, why people want to live here. Yet, you'll still encounter miles of farm country and quiet back roads where you can stop and enjoy the solitude. This ride is a good look at the changing nature of a rural countryside — one that is still relatively unspoiled by growth. Bring along some snacks and water for there are no stores along this route. Enjoy the road names along this ride — somehow Crooked Brook and Cheese Factory Road seem perfect for mountain biking — and they are.

How To Get There

Take Route 12 north from the intersection of the NYS Thruway. From the Riverside Mall, the start is about 8 miles north. Take the South Trenton exit off Route 12 and head west, coming to the divided street that marks South Trenton. Turn left (south) and turn left again just beyond the South Trenton Pub. Park at the Taft Community ball field. You might, if you are interested in history, make a note to check the burial ground that is right across the highway, behind the Presbyterian Church.

The Ride

From the ball field, pedal back down to the divided street and turn left. Cruise south. After crossing Ninemile Creek, continue on and watch for Coombs Road East which branches off to the left at Mile 1.5. This is a rough, narrow, tree-lined asphalt road with a few homes along it, quite typical of the roads you'll travel during this ride. After a little over a half mile, you'll coast down a shallow hill to a stop sign. This wider road is Crooked Brook Road.

Climb straight ahead up the winding road, being alert for traffic. You've got a steady mile of pretty tough climbing. Three-quarters of the way up, pass by W. Davis Road which veers of to the left. As you come to the main highway, continue the ascent, heading to the left, riding south on the wide shoulder. Continue climbing to Mile 3.8 and then, just as you are ready to head downhill, take the sharp left, just after the crest of the hill, marked as Miller Road.

Miller Road has a number of homes along it and looking off to the south at the great view, it is easy to see why. Pedal over Route 12 at Mile 4.5 and pass by the turn for Route 8 (Roberts Road), enjoying a short rolling downhill with hay fields on both sides. See the antennas on the top of those hills? That's where you'll be in a short while. At Mile 6.2, the road pitches down again with a right turn and another stop sign.

Turn right toward Utica. Pass the Town of Deerfield building and get primed for another steep downhill. Wowee!! A half-mile of paved descent, then a short climb, then another drop. Be careful with the traffic, the shoulder is quite narrow. At Mile 8.5, start another climb and just a quarter mile later, you'll see Bell Hill Road going off to the left. Take it.

This is another rough paved road that might have been better left to gravel. At Mile 9.3, you'll pass a dirt road that goes up to one set of antennae. Bear left and stay on pavement. (The old farm house here is all that remains of a once-working farm.) Get ready to climb.

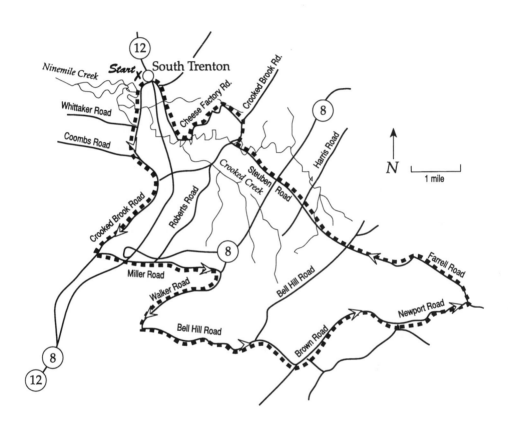

Ninemile Creek

Start

South Trenton

(12)

Whittaker Road

Coombs Road

Cheese Factory Rd.

Crooked Brook Rd.

(8)

Harris Road

N

1 mile

Crooked Brook Road

Roberts Road

Crooked Creek

Steuben Road

(8)

Miller Road

Walker Road

Bell Hill Road

Bell Hill Road

Brown Road

Newport Road

Farrell Road

(8)

(12)

This is the toughest section of the ride. Gear down and climb up past several homes which, as you get higher, have wonderful vistas out their front windows. At Mile 10, the climb lessens and at Mile 10.4, you are level again. Recover and cruise along to the next intersection. Turn left and get set for some more climbing. Are we having fun yet? This is a real "granny gear" climb of about a half mile which ends up at the antenna site.

(Note: At the top, Bell Hill Road which goes to the left of the tower changes to dirt and is marked "Dead End" at both ends. It may be worth exploring for it goes into a jeep trail. We did not take the bikes all the way through to where it comes down to Steuben Road.)

For this ride, take Brown Road and start down on pavement for a nice half-mile descent and then enjoy another drop through a residential area. At the Mile 12.2, you will come to the highway. Turn left and use the shoulder for the short climb and then let the bike fly as you lose much of the altitude you just gained. Let your momentum carry you up the next hill. Pass Timber Road on the left and after another moderate climb, you'll coast down past the Spain Gulf Road and turn left on the Newport Road (Mile 15.0) The tough riding is done — the rest of this is a piece of cake.

Curious onlookers along the Utica Hill Climb route.

Approaching Canary Farms on Farrell Road.

Newport Road is another of those bumpy narrow paved roads that weave through this area. There's some pretty farmland and easy riding — perfect for mountain bikes. After two miles of quiet riding, you'll drop sharply down to Farrell Road.

Turn left and climb up Farrell Road, past several handsome farms. After several miles (Mile 18.3), you'll be at the large dairy farm called Canary Farms. Continue on the same road, now marked as Steuben Road. Pedal along past field after field on this nice level road. At Mile 21.5, you'll come to Route 8 at the Town Highway Garage. Cross and proceed straight ahead.

You've got more rolling paved road ahead through farmland. After little more than a mile, you'll climb up to an intersection. Turn right and coast down, over the brook, and after a little climb, come to West Steuben Road on the left. (Mile 23.4)

Turn left and pedal down this country road, past a private airstrip — the hangar has a nice-looking Piper Cub in it — and watch for the sign for Cheese Factory Road. Check out the lovely homes in the woods to your right as you start down. Straight ahead in the distance you can see the traffic on Route 12. You'll like the way this road winds down to Ninemile Creek, crossing it with a one-lane bridge and then, just a half mile later, crosses it again with a wider bridge. Once you climb out of the creek crossing, you'll have a wide smooth ride back to the intersection with Putnam Road. (Mile 27.7)

Now it is just a left turn to cross under Route 12 and you are back to the South Trenton main drag. Turn left, cruise down to the turn for the park, and congratulate yourself — this has been a good mountain bike workout.

Syracuse Area Rides

Camillus Canal Cruise   18 miles
Beginner

Montezuma Swamp Tour   13.5 miles
Beginner -- Mix of dirt and pavement

Bear Swamp Romp   9 miles
Intermediate/Advanced

Happy Valley Circuit   13.5 miles
Beginner

Hewitt Forest Loop   9 miles
Intermediate

Stoney Pond Trek   9.5 miles
Intermediate -- all woods trails

Labrador Twin Loops   13 miles
Intermediate

The spectacular view from the hang glider launch point on Jones Hill.
(Labrador Twin Loops Ride)

Camillus Canal Cruise

18 miles

Beginner

Who hasn't sung "I've got a mule, her name is Sal, Sixteen miles on the Erie Canal...?" While your mule may be two-wheeled instead of four-legged, it's easy to visualize canal boats plying the route of this easy 18 mile ride through the heart of Central New York.

The Erie Canal was 350 miles long and stretched from Albany to Buffalo. A number of sections have been restored but none better than the starting point of this route at the Erie Canal Park in the Town of Camillus. Hundreds of volunteers have cleared the canal of trees, built dams, and filled the ditch with water. As you will find as you pedal west, other portions of the canal are dry and overgrown. Likewise, the towpath conditions varies depending on the energy of local volunteer groups.

Canal boat tours of this restored stretch are run on Sundays from May to October.

This is a great ride for new riders. It is flat and relatively smooth and being an out & back course, allows you to shorten it at any point. If you want more, the towpath is open to the west of Jordan or once back at the start, to the east to the Warners-Amboy Road.

Mosquitoes and horseflies are sometimes bothersome along this route — bring some repellent along.

How To Get There

From Syracuse, take Route 690 west toward Baldwinsville and at the State Fairgrounds, follow Route 695 toward Auburn. Stay on Route 5 toward Auburn and following the signs for the "Erie Canal Park," take the Camillus/Warners exit. At the stop, go right and take the next right to the park. There is plenty of parking near the restored Sims' store.

The ride starts at a restored site, Sims' store, which is located at the junction of Warners Road and the canal. It served as not only a general store and a departure station for persons riding the canal boats, but it also was a residence of John Sims and family. Local lore has it that Baby Susie's carriage rolled into the canal with Susie aboard, perhaps convincing John to move is family elsewhere. Today, there are many Sims families in the Camillus area.

Sims' Store marks the start of the ride.

The Ride

Head west from Sims' store, crossing Devoe Road and heading up the towpath on the right side of the canal. The riding is flat and smooth on a wide path as you pass the Camillus Gun Club. Then the trail narrows but it is well-kept and fast. Except for the lack of mule or horse droppings, it's not hard to visualize how active this

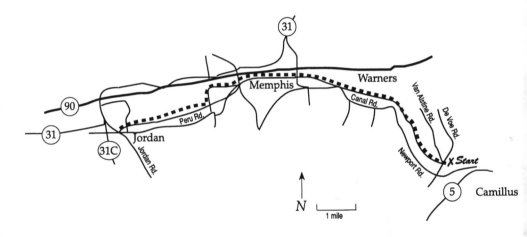

towpath once was. At Mile 2, you'll come to the end of the restored canal as you pass the park in the hamlet of Warners.

At Warners, cross behind the Brown Cow Cafe and follow the wide gravel road that is the old towpath but also is open to vehicles. Note that the canal reverts to its unimproved condition and now has more brush, stagnant water, and debris. It makes you appreciate even more the volunteer work in Camillus.

As you come to a dirt barrier and single track at Mile 3.0, notice the slate walls of the old canal. This stretch of towpath is not used as frequently and you can expect some underbrush and brambles. Persevere for the route comes out at Memphis, another canal town, at Mile 4.5.

You're close to the Thruway and will hear traffic as you pedal along toward the next hamlet, Peru. As you cross the paved road at Peru, you'll see that the towpath up ahead is blocked off by private homeowners. Jog right and then left onto Powerhouse Road and follow it west. After swinging south on the road, you will pick up the towpath again at Mile 7.

It will be easy riding all the way to Jordan on a more-improved path. You will pass the covered landfill at Mile 8 and soon arrive at the Elementary School in the Village. Cruise through the parking lot and pick up the canal again, which has been converted to a lovely park. Ride up to Main Street and take a look at some of the old buildings. Jordan was once a thriving canal town and then went through a long period of decline. It is now making a strong comeback. There is a restaurant as well as a grocery store for snacks before the return trip to Camillus.

Short trip option: For an easy 9 mile jaunt, head east from Sims Museum along the East Towpath Trail, crossing Nine Mile Creek as far as the Warners Road. Return to the start and continue west to Warners Park. Then reverse your course back to the Museum. This is a perfect ride for a group with new or young cyclists — it is flat, smooth, and interesting.

Montezuma Swamp Romp

15.7 miles

Beginner — Mix of dirt and pavement

This is an easy ride on dirt and pavement that starts and ends beside the Montezuma National Wildlife Refuge, one of the major nesting and feeding areas for migratory waterfowl in the Northeast. The 6,432 acre refuge is unique in that it is bisected by one of the country's busiest highways, the New York State Thruway. So, as you pedal along the route, tractor-trailers may roar in the distance, but you'll undoubtedly see Canada geese, great blue herons, and perhaps even a bald eagle. If you ride this route during the spring or fall migration periods, you'll see countless flocks of ducks and geese. Since this ride skirts a wildlife refuge, always yield the right of way to creatures with feathers or fur. (Note: bring a bike lock along so that you can take a short hike.)

The Refuge is administered by the U.S. Fish & Wildlife Service (315- 568-5987). There is an information center which is staffed in the summer and which has rest rooms and an observation platform. The Service has not permitted mountain bikes on Refuge roads and trails in the past so do not ride there without permission. The route described here skirts the Refuge on lightly-traveled public roads.

There are miles and miles of back roads in this area that are wonderful for cruising by mountain bike. Sprinkled with farms and homes, and both dirt and pavement, these tend to follow the north/ south orientation of the glacial terrain. This is easy riding and as you will see, very inviting for more "do it yourself" exploration.

How To Get There

The Refuge is about twenty miles west of Syracuse or five miles east of Seneca Falls on Route 20. From the NYS Thruway use Exit 41 and follow Route 318 five miles to Route 20. Turn left and head north on Route 89 for two miles. You will find a large parking area on the right (east) side of the road overlooking the Refuge. This is your starting point.

The Ride

While you are getting the bikes ready to go, why not look over the Refuge that lies down below you. You'll see some lovely meadows, the main marsh, and off to the southeast, the Visitors Center and observation tower.

Cross the road and turn left, heading south on the bike shoulder of Route 89. In just over a quarter mile, you'll see the Esker Brook Trail sign pointing off to the right. Take the paved road and climb past a lovely stone house. You'll see nesting boxes in the field as you climb up to the intersection.

Continue straight ahead on to the dirt road (Lay Road) and past several large farm fields. As you approach paved County Road 101, note the stately home surrounded by evergreens off to your right. Turn left on CR 101. (Mile 1.5)

Be careful of the quarter-mile on the County Road (there's no shoulder) and turn right on the narrow Nearpass Road. You'll cross several irrigation ditches on the flat dirt road as you head west.

At Mile 2.9, turn right on Middle Black Brook Road. Pedal past a lightly-populated area and climb up over the New York Thruway on a narrow bridge. Take the next left and scoot down a little drop, crossing White Brook and swinging up to the right to a maple-lined lane heading north. As you ride along, you'll traverse field after field of farmland which will be in corn some years, pasture in others.

Pass by Stevenson Road and be alert for a dog at Mile 5.0 coming off from your left. At West Tyre Road, turn right and swing down the little hill, taking the next left on Sutterby Road. This long dirt road takes you past the Town Clerks's office with a gentle climb before you drop down to Lamb Road at Mile 6.6.

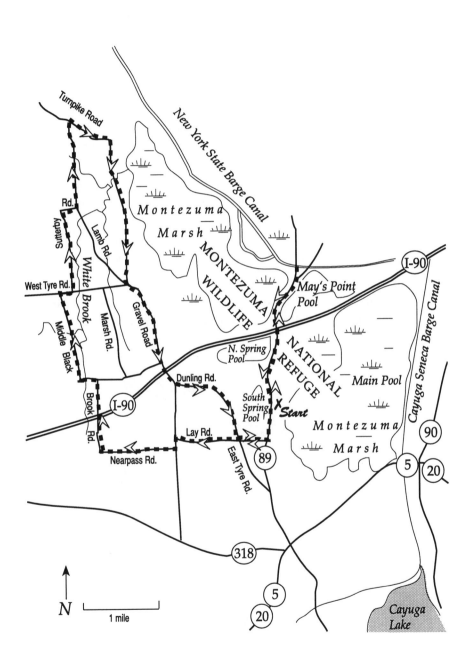

Lamb Road reminds one of "You take the high road..." lyrics as you ride past an interesting mix of lovely new homes next to abandoned farms on this elevated road. At Mile 7.7, carefully approach the drop to the intersection with Turnpike Road (County Road 105) and turn right, watching for traffic.

You'll have a little more traffic and several small climbs to deal with as you head east for a little less than a mile to Gravel Road, which of course is not gravel any longer. Turn right. (Mile 8.5)

Gravel Road will be easy riding on smooth pavement. Looking off to the right, you'll see that you are paralleling the route that you came north on. At Mile 10.5, you'll arrive at a four-way intersection marked by the Magee Volunteer Fire Department Building 2. Bear left and pedal through the little hamlet of Tyre, continuing straight ahead, climbing up over the Thruway at Mile 11.5.

Take the next left turn, Durling Road, which will lead you around to the Esker Brook Trail parking area. Here you have several options. You can lock up your bike and take a short two mile hike or you can continue back on the ride. (Mile 12.5)

Canada geese crossing the path on the Montezuma ride.

If you chose to walk for a bit, chain your bikes (Do not ride the Esker Trail!) The trail crosses the tiny brook and has a quick climb up to the ridge. (This is an esker, left by the glacier, from which the trail gets its name.) Walk north up to the small pond and take a moment at one of the overlook areas to watch for wildlife. Don't be surprised to see large carp cavorting about in the algae-rich water. It's easy to forget, in this tranquil spot, that the Thruway is just over the ridge. The trail back to the starting point is well-marked and easy traveling.

Bald eagles were raised at Tschache Pool.

Back at the Esker Trail parking area, turn left and let's head to Tschache Pond. Take East Tyre Road south to the intersection you passed on the way in. Turn left and cruise down to Route 89. Turn left and you'll find the parking area a half-mile ahead. Continue on another mile to check out more of the Refuge.

Bike north on the wide bike lane, again climbing up over the Thruway, to Tschache Pool which will be on your left (Mile 14.7).

Stop by the lookout tower and take the pedestrian walkway along the pool. This trail goes about 4 miles up to the tip of the pool but will likely be posted, during nesting season, against travel more than a few hundred yards. Be sure to observe any "no pedestrian traffic" signs. The flooded timber area of the Tschache Pool is a heron rookery. Take a moment and look over the pool — note the nests in the stark dead trees in the distance. Some of these were once used as bald eagle hacking sites. (In 1976, the Montezuma Refuge cooperated with the New York Department of Environmental Conservation to release eagles at Montezuma. Through 1980, 23 eagles were released through a "hacking" program. Since then, bald eagles have returned to Montezuma and have reared young.)

From Tschache pool, retrace your path on Route 89 south, using the wide shoulder as a bike lane. After a half mile, you will pass the North Spring Pool. Watch for nesting boxes in the woods off to your right as you pedal along this gentle road and in another half mile, carefully cross the highway back to your car.

Bear Swamp Romp

9 Miles

Intermediate/Advanced

Bear Swamp, long a favorite of cross country skiers and snow-mobilers, is a great place to mountain bike. This small state forest is an area of reforestation lying on a high ridge just west of Skaneateles Lake. A deep depression, the so-called Bear Swamp, runs through the middle of it while to the east is another high ridge which in turn pitches steeply down to the south end of Skaneateles Lake. All this adds up to an extensive system of trails and dirt road, steep hills, stream crossings, and mud — perfect setting for a mountain bike ride.

A youth group from Cortland designed and marked a 15 mile long ski trail which weaves through the State Forest on trails and dirt roads. (You will take a cutoff for this 9 mile ride.) This ride starts at an elevation of 1800' and after several miles of trails through the woods, descends down to Bear Swamp Creek (elevation 1520') and then climbs up the ridge on the east side to about 1800', descending again for a long climb back to the start. All turns are marked with red arrows tacked up on trees while the trail itself is marked with yellow D.E.C. medallions.

The nine mile course is difficult at times due to some steep climbs and descents and some creek crossings and mud: however, it does not require extensive all-terrain bike experience.

How To Get There

There are several entry points to Bear Swamp off Route 41A. For this ride, begin just behind the Colonial Lodge, a restaurant which calls itself "Bear Swamp's Living Room." Parking is available on the dirt access road just behind the lodge.

From the Village of Skaneateles, take Route 41A south 16 miles starting out along the west side of Skaneateles Lake. Continue through New Hope and several miles ahead, you'll find the parking area on a sweeping curve of the highway. From the south, take Route 41 from Homer north and follow the signs for Route 41A. Climb through the hamlet of Sempronius and look for the Colonial Lodge on the right. It is 10 miles from Homer Village to the start.

The ride starts with a left turn into the woods opposite the road sign.

The Ride

The trail begins with a left turn into the woods just as you start east on Hartnett Road. (The road has a "Seasonal Use Road" sign at the start.) As soon as you enter the forest, be ready for another left turn marked with red turn arrows and a yellow metal markers. The

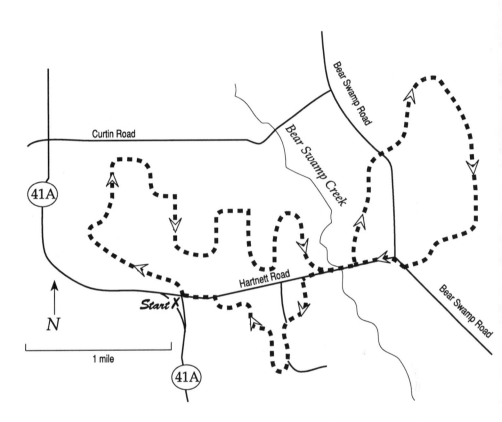

Curtin Road

Bear Swamp Road

Bear Swamp Creek

41A

Hartnett Road

Bear Swamp Road

Start X

N

1 mile

41A

first mile is flat trail on pine needles with small stream crossings, most of them dry in summer. Here's an early test of your bike-balancing ability as you try to negotiate the wooden bridges with their narrow slats. As you pedal along through a section of hard-woods, you may be able to hear traffic on Route 41A off to your left. Re-enter the pine plantation and ride a shady half mile through it as you approach Mile 2. So far, it's been a piece of cake. If you have had mechanical problems, there's a cutoff trail just after Mile 2 that brings you back to the starting point.

After a nice quarter mile downhill at Mile 2.5, you will have a sharp right turn into the woods. (Watch for this one — the red arrows come up on you fast as you steam downhill.) Then, crank through a series of rolling climbs and descents and you will soon connect with a trail favored by all-terrain vehicles and dirt bikes. It is time to get muddy — this section gets pretty chewed up. After a short stretch, climb back up to an outlet on Hartnett Road, about halfway down the hill. Turn left and enjoy a quick drop down across Bear Swamp Creek. The trail will turn sharply to the left as you climb up the rise on the other side. This is Mile 4.

Get ready to climb. After a stream crossing and a short steep uphill through some brambles and berries, you might ponder about how Bear Swamp got its name. Thoughts of berry-picking bruins should motivate you up the gradual climb to Bear Swamp Road. Cross the road and pick up the trail which continues up a road used by four-wheeled vehicles. This is the toughest portion of the ride — the road not only is steep, it also goes on for a half mile. With the steepness and the loose gravel, you'll likely have to dismount and walk up several sections. Take your time. Just when you think you are at the top, you'll round a corner and have to climb some more. Mile 5 is at the top of the hill.

From Mile 5 to Mile 6, the dirt road usually has lots of mud holes filled with stagnant water. Most can be circumnavigated in the woods. The riding is challenging due to the clay road and the slippery sections, even in dry weather. Motor vehicles keep it quite torn up. After a mile of slipping and sliding, watch for a right turn into the woods just after the 6 mile mark. Navigate along the ridge, following the markers, staying alert for the cutoff trail, marked with red medallions, going off to the right. You'll spot it just after a short descent. This cutoff soon intersects with the main trail (you are cutting off about six miles) and starts a long downhill, complete with some rocky stream crossings, back to Bear Swamp Road. This is the best downhill section — keep your weight over the back wheel and let the bike run.

The turns are well-marked with arrows and medallions.

At the road, turn right and pedal several hundred yards to the intersection with Hartnett Road. Turn left and cruise down across the creek. As you look up ahead, you can see the climb that lies ahead of you. If you are pressed for time, you can climb straight up (Well, it is nearly straight up!) Hartnett Road to the parking area. For this route, turn left shortly after starting the climb up Hartnett. There's a clearing that looks like the trail just before the turn so watch for the yellow trail markers.

The climb back is steady and dry with several "get off and push" sections. About halfway up the hill, there's a breather as you pedal a level section and then there is one short climb to Mile 8. (The marker, because of the cutoff, says 14.) The last half mile is a slight uphill climb through the hardwoods, a winding trail that tests your single-track riding ability, especially when tired. When you intersect Hartnett, turn left, and after several hundred yards, you will be back at the starting point — a little more tired and muddy than when you started. Why not try the whole 15 mile trail next time?

Happy Valley Circuit

13.5 miles

Beginner

The 8,645 acre Happy Valley Wildlife Management Area consists of land that once was cleared and intensely farmed. During the Depression in the 1930's, the Federal Resettlement Administration bought up a number of failed farms — which formed the initial acreage for the area. During this ride, you'll see many of the stone walls and apple and sugar maple trees that mark the old farmsteads.

The Happy Valley Circuit begins with a stretch on paved highway and then covers a rolling loop of woods roads featuring some moderate climbs. It is suitable for novice riders.

Bring a map and compass for there are many side trails and Jeep roads in this area which you may wish to explore. Being a wildlife management area, this tract attracts score of hunters during big game season so avoid the area during the late fall.

How To Get There
From Route I-81, take the exit for Route 104 and head east for 5.5 miles. At Mosher Corners, you'll see the D.E.C. field office on the right. Ample parking is available opposite the office.

The Ride
From the parking site, bike out to Route 104 and turn right, heading down the hill. This first stretch is on a well-traveled highway with no bike lane so ride with care on the right side.

Right away, you'll pass the outlet from Mosher Pond at the base of the first hill. This is one of three impoundments built in the late 1930's by Civilian Conservation Corps and Works Progress Administration forces. You'll see the other two impoundments before the ride is through.

As you climb, note the mature stands of conifers that were also planted by the CCC and WPA crews. Continuing straight ahead past Albion Road on the paved highway, you will pass an unimproved woods road on the right at Mile 1.6 that is a possibility for further exploration. (It is passable in most spots but has some very wet areas which will require you to lug your bike for a bit. It joins this route down near Whitney Pond.) Continue on Route 104 until you come to the D.E.C. sign for Happy Valley Wildlife Management Area at Mile 2.6.

Happy Valley provides an easy introduction to dirt road riding.

Turn south on the "Seasonal Use Highway" road, also known as the Happy Valley Road, and start a short climb on the smooth dirt road. You'll soon see that the area is marked by a wide variety of hardwoods and softwoods in all stages of maturity. Lumbering

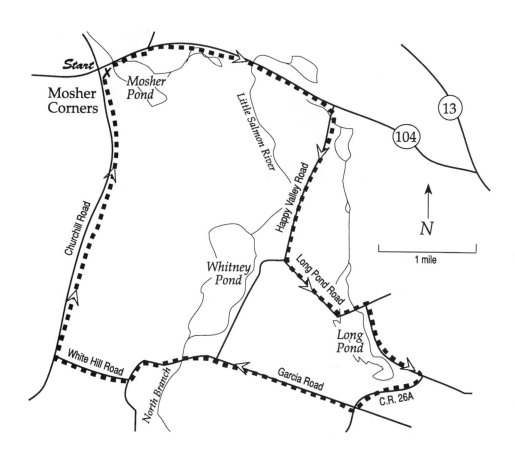

An inviting dirt road leads you into the Wildlife Managegment Area.

operations may well be going on. The route continues straight ahead for several miles although you will pass several side trails. After a mile on dirt, you'll pass a narrow road going off to the left — continue straight ahead and expect some potholes and ruts. Like so many of the rides on state land, this one passes by a mixture of public and private land. At Mile 4, a gated road on your right heads to a private parcel — it also connects with the unimproved road that we passed on Route 104. Continue straight ahead.

Just ahead, you'll pass a private camp that was once a schoolhouse and shortly afterward, come to a major dirt intersection at Mile 4.2. The Happy Valley Road, which you will link up with later, goes to the right. You should turn left on the unmarked Long Pond Road. After passing a cemetery which has some old markers of some of the original farmers, you'll have a half mile of easy clay road riding and soon arrive at Long Pond at Mile 5. This is another of the impoundments constructed during the Depression.

Cross over the levee in the middle of the pond and at the top of the short hill on the opposite side, turn right. You'll have some easy riding in the shade through the hardwoods as you parallel Long Pond. After a delightful downhill, you will arrive at a paved road, County Route 26A.

Turn right and enjoy some smooth downhill cruising on this lightly-traveled road. At Mile 7, take the dirt road that climbs to the right. This is Garcia Road which has a number of private camps (and a few private eyesores) along it. After a half-mile of level riding on the rough road, you'll start a moderate climb. At the top, note the old stone wall and the gnarled old sugar maples lining the road. Pedalling on, you'll come to a boggy area dammed by beavers and, at Mile 8.7, arrive at the junction with Happy Valley Road.

Long Pond was built by the Civil Conservation Corps in the 1930's.

Just ahead, as you come down a hill, there's a parking area on the right which overlooks the outlet from Whitney Pond. You may wish to stop and ride, or walk, down to the spillway. Continuing down the hill, you'll cross the outlet which is the North Branch of the Little Salmon River.

Climb up the steep hill ahead for about a quarter-mile and then, at Mile 9.5, the road that you passed back on Route 104 will come in from the right. Start down the nice little downhill run but get ready to turn right on the unmarked White Hill Road. If you look straight ahead as you start down White Hill, you can see the climb facing you on the other side of the creek. After a a long steady descent, climb steeply for about a quarter of a mile and then it is a short drop back down to the intersection with Churchill Road.

Turn right and it is three miles back to your parking area. Churchill Road is easy riding in most spots although you'll encounter some wet areas and rutted spots. The terrain is rolling and old stone fences line the road. At Mile 12 you'll pass a boggy area on the right and after huffing up a few last climbs, see the maintenance buildings that mark your starting point.

Hewitt Forest Loop

9 miles

Intermediate

Hewitt State Forest is relatively small and many of the roads and trails end on private property. This loop starts in the Forest, drops down to a paved secondary road, and then has a long steady climb back up to the top of the ridge. There are many options for exploring trails in the Forest after the ride.

How To Get There

From Skaneateles, take East Lake Road (Route 41) south past Spafford. As you pass the south end of Skaneateles Lake and head down a long downhill, watching for Ripley Road. Hewitt Road is just ahead on the left.

From Homer, follow Route 41 north past the hamlet of Scott. Hewitt Road will be on the right a quarter mile after a new white church. Hewitt Road is a steep climb for nearly a mile. Park at the four-way intersection.

The Ride

From the parking site, continue on Hewitt Road which will pitch down and after a left turn, continue on a nice little downhill crossing Callan Creek at Mile .5. (A seasonal road goes off to the right — remember that for a jaunt at the end of the ride.) Continue up the short steep climb straight ahead through private land and then you are back in State Land with groves of mature evergreens shading the road.

Hewitt Road now descends steadily and as it crosses a tributary of Cold Brook, swings sharply right and continues down until it intersects the paved Cold Brook Road at Mile 1.8. This is a great downhill — remember it when you are climbing back up on to the plateau later on. As you make the right turn on Cold Brook Road, notice the signs and fencing for the deer farm.

Head south on Cold Brook Road being careful to watch for traffic. There is a shoulder to ride on in spots but be alert during this segment of the ride. The paved road is relatively level and easy riding. Look off to the right and you can see the high land from which you just descended.

At Mile 3.0, a seasonal road goes off to the left and you may note a private road to the right that dips into the valley and climbs straight up the mountain. Continue straight ahead on pavement. At Mile 4.0, just after you cross Callan Brook, the seasonal road goes straight ahead as the paved road turns left. Take the rutty seasonal road for a mile stretch of interesting riding.

Heading home on snow-covered Brake Hill Road.

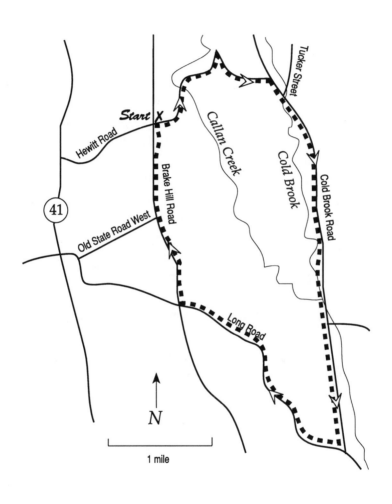

An old cemetery is on your right as you start up the jeep trail. There will likely be wet spots and even water in the road from the runoff on the farmland up on the right side of your route. Ignore the several farm roads that head uphill and continue ahead. You'll probably hear traffic on the road below you as you parallel the pavement. The trail ends with a sharp downhill pitch ending back on the paved road.

Just ahead, with a mobile home park on the left, turn right on Long Road which you will soon find, should be named Long Hill Road. You may have some canine company as you start up Long Road but they are just barkers. The first climb is over a mile long with farm fields on both sides. After a left turn, you'll start another extended climb through hardwoods until you level off just after Mile 7.0. Brake Hill Road, a seasonal road, intersects at Mile 7.5. Turn right and head back toward the parking area.

The last segment is level, with nice views off to both sides, as you ride along the crest of the hill. Just after Mile 8.0, the Old State Road comes up from the left. Continue straight ahead on the jeep trail and enjoy the easy riding back to the starting point. You will again enter state forest land as you near your ending point.

Since this is a short loop, you may want to play a bit when you get back. You might take the "Dead End" road continuation of Brake Hill Road for over a mile north for some excellent views or you might want to head back down the shady jeep trail that goes down Callan Brook. There are several other forest trails to explore as well.

Stoney Pond Trek

9.5 miles

Intermediate — all woods trails

Located just 28 miles from Syracuse and 32 miles from Utica, Stoney Pond State Forest is an undiscovered gem for Central New York mountain biking. The state constructed a number of cross country ski trails in the late 1980's that are perfect for off-road biking. This is a compact area, only 1469 acres in size, but the well-planned trails run through lovely plantations of red, white, and scotch pines and wind among hardwood forests of sugar and red maple, black cherry, white ash, and beech.

The 44 acre Stoney Pond was constructed in the late 1950's as a wildlife habitat. Camping is permitted in the area for up to three days without a permit.

Except for the pond, which can be driven to, this area has little usage after the snow melts. Because of this, the trails can be clogged with brambles so you should wear jeans or long socks for leg protection. The terrain is rolling but there are numerous stretches of boggy riding that will provide technical challenges.

This is a good place for beginners to get their bikes dirty without facing steep hills or mud. For a beginner's ride, pedal down to Stoney Pond and circle the pond using Trail 2, then Trail 1.

How To Get There

From the Syracuse area, take Route 20 from Cazenovia to Nelson. Continue east for 3.4 miles to Willowvale Road. Turn right and head south to Old State Road. Turn right again heading west for about a half mile to Jones Road. Turn left (south) and after the road turns to dirt, you'll enter the state forest. There are two parking areas — continue past the first one and a half mile later, you'll come to the second one. You should see the "Trail 1" marker on the east side of the road.

From the east, take Route 20 to Morrisville. Continue west for 3 miles and look for the Willowvale Road on the left. Follow the directions above.

From the south, take Route 12B from Sherburne north to Earlville. Go west at the light to the "T" intersection, then turn right and drive about 8 miles to Route 26 in Eaton. Turn left on 26 to West Eaton, bearing right on County Road 52. Take the second right on to Tuscarora Road. Curve left to stay on Tuscarora and take the second right on to Jones Road. The parking area will be on the right.

The Ride

This ride has two components: a five mile loop on the ski trails to the west and then, after a return to the parking area, a 4.5 mile loop around Stoney Pond.

From the parking area, cross the road and head west on Trail 11. As you climb gently on the path, you'll get an early taste of the area as you pass by a stately grove of tall pines. Notice how still it is.

Right away, Trail 8 will head off to the right but continue on Trail 11, biking down by an old stone wall. After a brief climb, you'll have some nice woods riding with a few technical challenges thrown in by roots and rocks. This is perfect mountain bike riding. Pass by Trail 20 (left) and Trail 9 (right) and continue up through a pine grove. After some easy riding on pine needles, you'll come to the intersection with Trail 12. Turn left.

This will be a long descent, with a few wet spots and areas of brambles thrown in for good measure. At the bottom, Trail 13 will come in from the left but continue straight, through a wet section of trail, until you come out on the logging road at Mile 1.5.

Turn left and follow the road as it winds up to the right. If there has been recent activity, you'll have plenty of muddy spots to

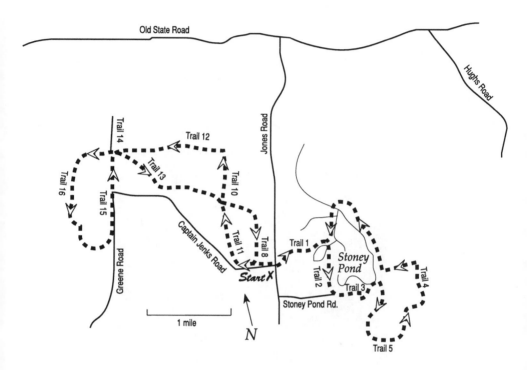

negotiate. Continue on the road, which is marked with yellow medallions, until it pitches down to the right. You'll see Trail 16 ahead. Get ready for some underbrush - - this is an area that sees few riders or hikers.

Plunge through the prickers — in late summer they can be handle-bar high. You'll soon be rewarded for your efforts by a ride through a corridor of tall trimmed fir trees. At Mile 2.5, you'll emerge from the woods at an old farm road. Turn left and follow Trail 15 up the hill past some pretty upland meadows and hay fields.

A corridor of stately fir trees at Mile 2.5.

As you re-enter State Forest at Mile 3, the route gets more difficult due to wet conditions. After a short battle with ruts and mud, you'll be back at the logging road. Turn right at once, retracing your route on Trail 12.

After just a few hundred yards, bear right on Trail 13. As you slog through a half-mile of soggy riding, it's easy to understand why the early settlers abandoned their farms in this area. Turning left on Trail 20, you'll start climbing out of the wet areas and end up with a pretty stretch through pines to the junction with Trail 11.

Turn left and pedal up to the next intersection, taking the right on to Trail 9. This will be gently downhill riding through hardwoods that have been recently logged. At Mile 4.5, you'll meet Trail 8 and bear right, enjoying a great descent through conifers. There are just enough roots to make you keep your speed down but it is a nice run. At the junction with Trail 11, turn left and cruise back to the parking area.

The ride continues on Trail 1. Pitch down the hill, noting how more worn these trails are. Follow Trail 1 to the first small impoundment and ride over the berm, taking the trail to the right (Trail 2). This is easy riding along a smooth jeep trail. You'll see Stoney Pond off to the left through the trees.

As you come out on to Stoney Pond Road, bear left and cruise down the left fork past a number of campsites lining the pond. At the barrier, ride down to the berm and pedal across it, stopping to admire the 44 acre lake. (Mile 6) There are sure to be Canada Geese nearby. A number of them stay here year-round — it's easy to see why.

The next stretch is the toughest of the ride due to brambles and roots. Push your bike up the far bank and take the trail that climbs straight ahead.

Trail 4 will go off to the right through the hardwoods. Plunge in and before long, you'll be at Trail 5 from which you can see the outlet brook from Stoney Pond.

At the intersection with Trail 4, which pitches downhill, bear right and follow it up and around to the intersection with Trail 6 and Trail 3. Turn left and cruise down to the intersection with Trail 1.

Looking west at Stoney Pond from Trail 1.

Turn right. It's all fun from here on home.

Trail 1 is well-worn from anglers and is an easy shaded ride. You'll pass a number of campfire spots and have some pretty views of the pond. After crossing three wooden bridges over incoming streams (dry in summer), you'll come again to the small impoundment. Retrace your route, climbing back up to the parking area.

Labrador Twin Loops

13 miles

Intermediate

The Morgan Hill State Forest, like its neighbor to the east, Highland Forest, is a favorite with Syracuse-area outdoor enthusiasts. You will likely share the trail, especially on the weekend, with hikers and other mountain bikers.

The terrain is a geologist's delight with hills and hollows running north & south. These "U-shaped" valleys, formed by glacial activity, are called "through valleys." There are several downhill ski areas (Labrador and Toggenburg) located on the eastern slopes of the hills.

This ride features some great single-track riding, a spectacular vista, a hair-raising descent down a western-style access road, and ends with a long descent It has several steep "dismount and push" uphill sections.

How To Get There

From I-81, take the Tully exit (14) and head east on Route 80 through Tully and Apulia Station. Look for Herlihy Road on the right just after the Agway Research Farm. Turn right and park near the intersection. You will see a Finger Lakes Trail sign on a pole marking the starting point.

The Ride

Head up Herlihy Road, which will turn to dirt just past a large farm, and start a steady climb. In just less than a mile, just after you pass an apple orchard on the right, you'll see the Finger Lakes Trail sign in the woods on the left.

The next half-mile is as much a hike as a ride. It is a steady climb, with lots of roots and logs, but with some sections which can be ridden. Be careful about spinning out on roots and leaving knobby scars on the trail — it is fragile in this area due to to heavy usage by hikers.

After a climb through hardwoods, you'll enter the spruce stands higher up and have better going. (Note how the spruce seedlings are fighting for survival as they are shaded by their parents.) Cross over a woods road, following the orange blazes. You'll reach the top of Fellows Hill (elevation 2019') at Mile 1.9. Shortly ahead, after a pretty stretch of single-track riding, you'll emerge onto an old wagon road. Turn right and enjoy some downhill riding. You have earned it.

Watch for the orange blazes marking the trail as you pedal along. The FLT route changes as permissions from landowners change and sometimes you'll see old blazes that are faded and no longer in effect. Follow the signs for a stretch of single-track off the woods road and then, after returning to the road, you will have a quick descent on the road. Be alert for a turn as the trail bears right into the woods and pitches straight down the hill on a trail made a bit tricky in parts by ruts and washouts. At Mile 3.2, after the descent, you'll come out on a Herlihy Road again. Follow the blazes to the left and you'll be at the Spruce Pond impoundment at Mile 3.3. About now you will realize that you could have driven up here — but then, later on, you would miss the great downhill ending to the ride.

Proceed on by crossing over the berm of Spruce Pond and head up the path. This section of the trail is even more heavily used since it is so accessible by auto. You'll have to carry your bike up a steep, but mercifully-short, hill. Once on top, you will find some good single-track riding on the worn path followed by a long gentle drop

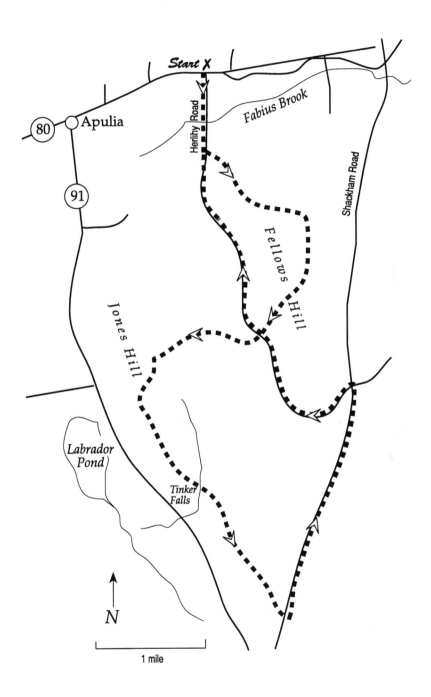

Start X

Fabius Brook

Herlihy Road

80 Apulia

91

Shackham Road

Fellows Hill

Jones Hill

Labrador
Pond

Tinker
Falls

N

1 mile

across private lands to a small brook. (Mile 4.3)

Climb up from the brook and you'll have some easy trail riding to the Jones Hill summit. As the trail swings left, you can get peeks through the foliage of a wonderful view but you feel cheated since you can't see that much until, at Mile 4.8, you suddenly emerge at a hang glider takeoff point. What a view! Nearly straight down is Labrador Pond, a kettle pond left by the glacier. To the right is the Apulia Station area and further north, more of Onondaga County.

If the weather is good, you'll be reluctant to move on. The Finger Lakes Trail heads along the rim but you should pedal out the access road. After some level riding, you will have a very steep winding descent down to Route 91. Work on your downhill riding as you enjoy this wonderful descent, keeping your weight back, avoiding skids on the loose shale. You will arrive at Route 91 at Mile 5.8. Turn left.

Just ahead, you'll see the parking area and access trail for Tinkers Falls. Tinkers Falls is a 20' waterfall off a ledge that is a nice example of one of the "hanging falls" created by the glacier. The trail in along the brook, well-worn by hikers, is less than a half mile. It's definitely worth an exploratory ride.

Continuing, cruise along the wide shoulder of the pavement for a little over a mile. Just as you see the slopes of Labrador Mountain ski area and start a downhill run, turn left up Shamrock Brook road.

After a brief climb, you'll have some easy back road riding and enter state land again at Mile 7.5. Pedaling along through tall spruces, you probably will hear logging activity and see neatly stacked piles of pulp logs. At the intersection at Mile 9.4, turn left and climb the hill.

This is the last climb and while only 200 feet or so in elevation, it comes when legs are tired. Shift down and get up on the pedals for a change of muscles, or push the bike. Once on top, it's easy dirt road riding back to Spruce Pond (Mile 10.7).

From Spruce Pond, you will have a steady descent on Herlihy Road to the parking spot. What a great ending to a challenging mountain bike workout.

Norwich Area Rides

Pharsalia Fling   11 miles
Beginner -- dirt roads with some moderate climbs.

Whaupaunaucau Forest Tour   7 miles
Intermediate -- trails and dirt forest roads

Brookfield Truck Trail Loop   11 miles
Intermediate -- Forest Truck Trails

Baker Forest Loop   10 miles
Intermediate/Advanced -- Hilly horse trails and forest roads

An abandoned farmhouse along the Pharsalia Fling route.

Pharsalia Fling

11 miles

Beginner — dirt roads with some moderate climbs.

After an initial climb into the Wildlife Management Area, you'll have shaded dirt road riding with a side trip to Bear Wallow Pond. The ride ends with two miles of downhill back to the car.

Because this is a wildlife area, there is very little development and few signs — it is left quite natural. Don't be surprised to see work details of prisoners from nearby Camp Pharsalia doing maintenance work in the Wildlife Management Area.

How To Get There

From Norwich on Route 12, take Route 23 west to North Pharsalia. Park on the south side of the highway on the ample shoulder opposite the large farm in the center of the hamlet.

From Route 81, exit at Whitney Point and follow Route 26 to Lower Cincinnatus and then Route 23 to North Pharsalia.

The Ride

Head east (toward Norwich) on the wide shoulder of Route 23 and after a quarter mile, you will come to an unnamed dirt road that is marked with a "Pharsalia Wildlife Management Area" sign. Turn left and start the steep climb up through an orchard of apple trees.

After a half mile climb, you will be on top and riding through groves of maples on a Jeep trail. At Mile 1, pedal past an abandoned farm house and the state land begins just ahead.

This is perfect mountain bike terrain: the road is rutted and often marked with loose rocks and gravel and there are just enough dips and climbs to make it interesting riding. Pass by a private road on the right at Mile 1.7 and start down a nice little run. Note the stands of mature evergreens on the left. You'll see plenty of these majestic stands before you are done.

Bear to the right at the intersection at Mile 2 and cruise through the spruces on smooth level road to the next intersection. (Mile 2.6) Note the gnarled old maples lining both sides of the road just prior to the junction.

Head straight down the hill and right away you will come to the unmarked Pigeon Hill Road. Turn left. As you pedal along, ignore the road coming down from the left and continue straight ahead, passing by another private dwelling. There's a cemetery with a well-built slate wall around it on the left as you climb up from the creek crossing and just beyond, a sharp left turn up the hill on Cole Hill Road. (Mile 3.4)

Bear Wallow Pond.

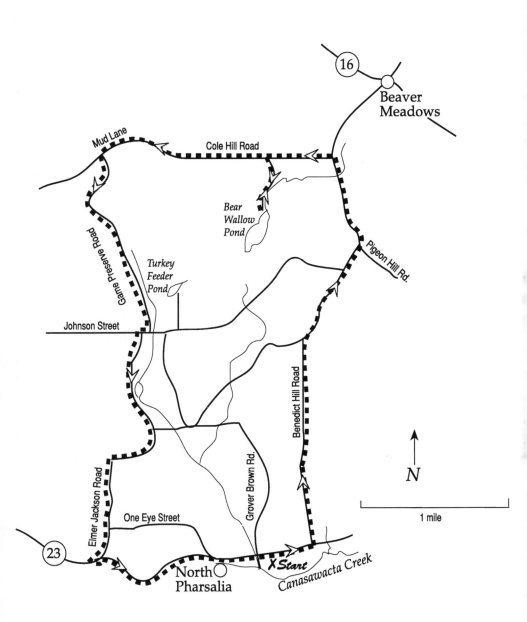

The climb is steep but mercifully short and soon you are pedaling easily on another road lined with maple trees. At Mile 4, turn left and ride the gentle half mile to visit Bear Wallow Pond. Bears or no bears, it's a pretty little pond with dark tannin-colored water.

When you return to Cole Hill Road at Mile 5, turn left and continue west. The next mile is easy mountain bike riding on a level dirt road. When you come to the unmarked intersection at Mile 6.3, turn left and cruise down Preserve Road. The next five miles are going to be fun.

Preserve Road is smoother than the roads you have been on. It drops gradually, passing a series of weirs which were built in the Civilian Conservation Corps days to control the brook. At Mile 7.9, at the intersection with Johnson Road, bear right and then take a quick left, continuing your southerly jaunt toward Route 23.

Lo and behold, you'll pass our old friend from other rides, the Finger Lakes Trail. Save that for another day. Continue ahead and pass by a larger impoundment. At Mile 8.7, you will have your next-to-last climb, a brief one, and then swing down past a beaver pond.

The last mile is a steeper drop. As you descend, you'll be able to see the traffic on Route 23 up ahead. After one last little climb up to the highway at Mile 10, it's an easy trip home.

Cross the highway carefully and turn left, enjoying the cooling descent back to North Pharsalia.

Whaupaunaucau Forest Tour

7 miles

Intermediate — trails and dirt forest roads

Whaupaunaucau means "Land of the marten" and while the marten has gone the way of the early settlers who used to inhabit this hill, the 1100 acre State Forest offers some great mountain biking — and a good chance of a glimpse at a deer or a wild turkey. A complex of trails, marked for cross country skiing with the yellow disks of the New York DEC, invite exploration. This route traverses the perimeter of the forest and combines trail riding with some stretches of dirt road. There are some good climbs and technical sections. Several trails may be difficult for the beginning rider.

How To Get There

Whaupaunaucau State Forest lies just off Route 320 to the northeast of Norwich. From Norwich, take Route 12 north to the Route 320 blinking light and go six miles. You will see the State Forest sign on the right. Take a left on Post Road and follow it up to the parking area. (Note: There is a lower parking area with a gate. If the gate is closed, park here and bike up the hill. If the road is open, drive the quarter mile up the hill and park in the area at the top. The ride will start here.)

From the north, drive south on Route 12 from Sherburne for 3.2 miles, turning left on Bryant Road. Follow Bryant for 2.4 miles until you come to Route 320. Turn right and the forest sign is just down the hill. Post Road will be a right turn.

The Ride

Pedal out of the parking area west, toward the small body of water that you can see through the trees. The trail should be marked "4" and be blazed with DEC yellow markers. The route goes across the top of the earthen dam and bears to the right along the edge of the impoundment. What a pretty start! Notice the stark dead spruce trees in the upper reaches of the pond.

As you head up from the pond, the trail will climb gradually and you'll encounter some wet spots as well as some rocky sections. At the top where the trail forks, bear to the left and you'll soon come to a dirt forest road. Continue across the road up toward the shale pit.

Just as you start up into the pit, the trail will go off sharply to the left and immediately start to climb — watch for it and shift down before you get to it. This is Trail "5" which has some interesting single-track riding. After the initial climb and some pretty woods riding, you'll come to another forest road at Mile 1.1. Turn left.

After a quarter-mile ride, you'll arrive at a trail on the right marked "7". Climb gently up through some mixed hardwood forest which is interspersed with some large white pines. Watch for the yellow markers if the trail is overgrown. It will bear left through a stand of evergreens and come out on another stretch of dirt road. Turn right and cruise down to the turn-around.

Continue straight ahead and after a short downhill, you'll come to an intersection with both trails marked "9". Turn right. Trail 9 starts off on an old logging road and after a quarter mile, bears off to the left on a narrow single-track. You'll like the easy downhill through the woods. At the bottom, the trail goes sharply left and is marked with an arrow. This is wild country — I like to look in the muddy sections for animal tracks — there are more of those than people or bike tracks.

After you cross a small dry creek with a wooden bridge, bear right and you will come to an intersection with Trail "10". Turn right and enjoy another downhill followed, at Mile 3.0, by a steady climb. As you climb on Trail "10", keep a watch for the turn off to

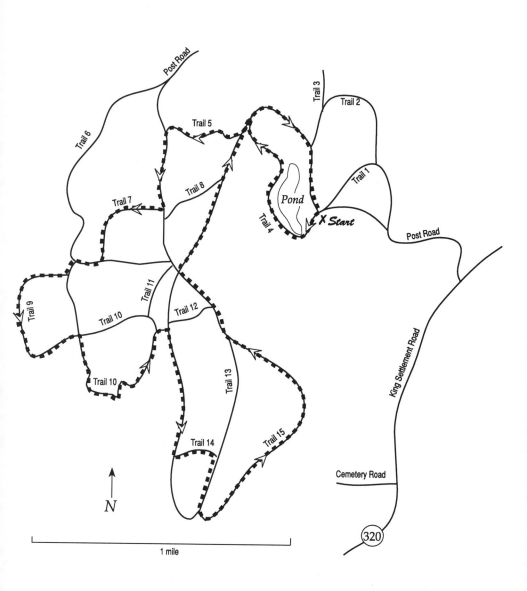

Post Road

Trail 3

Trail 2

Trail 5

Trail 6

Trail 8

Trail 1

Trail 7

Pond

Trail 4

X Start

Post Road

King Settlement Road

Trail 11

Trail 9

Trail 10

Trail 12

Trail 13

Trail 10

Trail 14

Trail 15

Cemetery Road

N

320

1 mile

the right. You will take that, cross another creek bed, and be at a forest road.

At the dirt road, turn right for some easy riding. After a half mile cruise, Trail "14" will be marked with an arrow on the left. Use this short grassy ride through pines to cut across to Trail "13". At the next junction, turn right and coast down on the grassy trail. You will come to Trail "15" just after Mile 4.0. Turn left.

This is another neat downhill, a little rocky in spots, that follows the contour lines down. Off to the right, you may be able to hear or see the traffic on Route 320. You will come out on an opening where you can see several lovely meadows and pastures. This view, along with the old apple trees, gives you a better idea of the overgrown farmland through which you have been riding.

Now you are going to gain back most of the elevation you have been enjoying on the downhills. Trail 15 climbs up fairly steeply with lots of cobbles to make the riding even more challenging. If you are tired, just push the bike — the climb is about a half mile. As you near the top, take the trail straight ahead. Some "Posted" signs along here mark the private land holdings, and you may spot a log cabin in the woods as you pass. Continue straight ahead on Trail "13" and after a quick little climb, you'll come to a forest road intersection at Mile 5.6. Bear to the right.

The rest of the ride is on forest road. It's an easy riding with a couple of minor climbs and a long downhill. If you're still game to ride some more, there are several more well-marked ski trails to explore right across from your parking spot.

Brookfield Truck Trail Loop

11 miles

Intermediate — forest truck trails

A hilly ride on dirt truck trails winding through Baker State Forest. This area contains over 100 miles of horse trails including 20 miles of forest roads which provide wide shady corridors for mountain biking.

How To Get There

From the west on Route 20, take Route 46 south to Hamilton and continue on Route 12B South to Earlville. Turn left and take East Main Street for a mile to Reece Road. Turn right and immediately bear left up Castle Hill and continue to Route 12. Turn right (south) on Route 12 and after a quarter of a mile, turn left on Knapp Road. Follow Knapp Road 3.5 miles until it intersects Chenango County Route 24 and continue straight ahead. After two miles, you will see the sign for "Charles Baker State Forest" and just up the hill ahead on the right, a large parking area.

From the east on Route 20, turn south in Bridgewater on Route 8 and proceed through Leonardsville and West Edmeston to the junction with County Route 25. Turn right (west) and in just over a mile, turn right again on County Route 24. Follow Route 24 for 4.5 miles and the parking area will be on the left at the top of a rise.

The Ride

From the parking area, head west down the hill on Route 24, being alert for traffic. Turn right into Baker Forest on Truck Trail 1 (TT1) which is wide and smooth with a shale base. Right away, a brief climb will introduce you to the hills of Chenango County. Furman Mills Road comes in on the left at Mile .8. That's the road upon which you will be returning at the end of the loop.

Off-road trails are closed from Oct 31 - May 1 in Baker State Forest.

Start a serious climb up past some private land. (In most state forests, there remain some enclaves of private lands and camps.) As you top the rise at Mile 1.4, you will find a lovely downhill run, straight as an arrow. This is what mountain biking is all about!

At Mile 1.7, the route comes to Truck Trail 7. Turn right and start a curved climb through large conifers. At Mile 2, the road starts

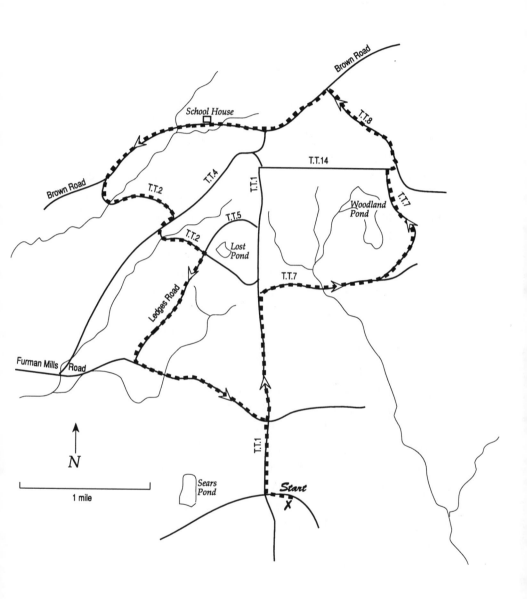

Brown Road

School House

T.T.8

Brown Road

T.T.2

T.T.4

T.T.1

T.T.14

Woodland
Pond

T.T.7

T.T.5

T.T.2

Lost
Pond

Ledges Road

T.T.7

Furman Mills Road

T.T.1

N

1 mile

Sears
Pond

Start
X

down on a great quarter-mile descent. By now you have gotten a taste of the ups and downs of the terrain throughout this loop. At Mile 3, pass by TT3 which deadends at a horse trail, and swing around to the left on TT7. This is nice shady riding, and you will come to another curving downhill run which ends at Mile 3.6. Note all the reforested areas with their ramrod straight pine trees.

Bear to the right at TT14 and immediately turn left at the intersection of Truck Trail 8 (Mile 3.9), enjoying a half mile of easy back road riding to the intersection with Brown Road. Turn left and start down, passing by TT12, for a long smooth downhill.

The route comes to a fork with Truck Trail 1 at Mile 5.3. If you are short of time, you can turn left and it will be three miles of climbs and descents back to the starting point. If you are up for more, continue downhill to the right on Brown Road and you will have another long smooth downhill run. At Mile 6, you will pedal past an old schoolhouse and just afterward, pass by an meadow. This stretch has many vestiges of the former farming activity — you'll agree as you ride past scores of ancient apple trees. A steady climb starts at Mile 6.5 and ends at Truck Trail 2 at Mile 6.8.

Turn left and descend down through the evergreens on TT2. Crossing the brook, get ready for a stiff climb up to TT4 at Mile 7.6. Turn right and just as you start down a long hill, turn left for a steep drop down across the brook on TT2. Keep your momentum up for you have a good climb at Mile 8.0. (Do you feel that you are always racing downhill or climbing in a granny gear?)

At the four-way intersection at Mile 8.3, your route goes sharply off to the right on Ledges Road. Before you swing down Ledges, you might, for a diversion, pedal up to the left on TT5. Just through the trees to the right, you'll see Lost Pond. Pedal on in and check it out. Across the road, if you follow the stream, there is a very pretty waterfall.

Back to business, and what a lovely business Ledges Road is as it gently drops for a mile. Note the rock outcroppings clearly visible off to the side. At Furman Mills Road, turn left and after a few last climbs and descents, you will intersect TT1 at Mile 10.5. Turn right and retrace your route back to the car.

Baker Forest Loop

10 miles

Intermediate/Advanced — Hilly horse trails and forest roads
Note: Off-road trails are closed to mountain bikes from October
31st to May 1st.

Baker State Forest has over 100 miles of horse trails as well as
20 miles of forest roads, all of which are great for mountain biking.
This ride combines single-track trails and undulating dirt roads to
provide a challenging ride.

How To Get There

From the west on Route 20, take Route 46 south to Hamilton
and continue on Route 12B South to Earlville. Turn left and take
East Main Street for a mile to Reese Road. Turn right and immediately bear left up Castle Hill and continue to Route 12. Turn right
(south) on Route 12 and after a quarter of a mile, turn left on Knapp
Road. Follow Knapp Road 3.5 miles until it intersects Chenango
County Route 24 and continue straight ahead. After two miles, you
will see the sign for "Charles Baker State Forest" and just up the hill
ahead on the right, a large parking area.

From the east on Route 20, turn south in Bridgewater on Route
8 and proceed through Leonardsville and West Edmeston to the
junction with County Route 25. Turn right (west) and in just over
a mile, turn right again on Chenango County Route 24. Follow
Route 24 for 4.5 miles and the parking area will be on the left at the
top of a rise.

The Ride

Note: There are a lot of horseback riders, and even llama trekkers on these trails. Remember, mountain bikers are much more mobile than mounted riders so walk the bike, let the horse folks by. Let's not wear out our welcome — they have been using these trails for decades.

From the parking area, head west down the hill on Route 24, being alert for traffic. Turn right on to Truck Trail 1 (TT1). As you arrive at the junction with Furman Mills Road, look on the right for the horse trail marked "17" going directly into the woods. As soon as you head down the single-track, you'll get a taste of the technical nature of this route as you work your way over many tree roots and encounter sections of trail chewed up by horses' hoofs. At the first little intersection, follow the signs to the lean-to. (Mile 1.2)

You'll enjoy some lovely "through the woods" riding and then, as you approach the brook, find that the riding gets trickier. There is a short technical section where you'll have to dodge some water bars and ride along the creek's bed. Look for the sharp left turn where Trail 17 heads up toward the lean-to. (Mile 1.9)

The lean-to on Trail 17 has adjacent horse barns.

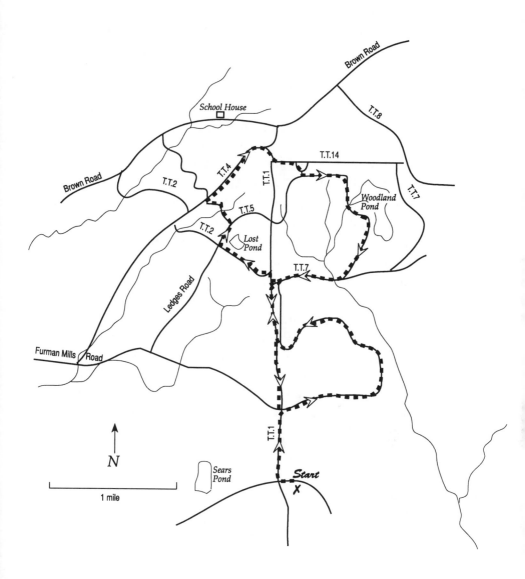

At Mile 2 you'll come to your first "push-the-bike" section of rutty uphill. Not only is it steep and blocked by diagonal water bars, the clay underpinning of the trail is often badly cut up by horses. As you puff up to the top, stop for a moment and note the old slate stone wall marking a former farm field.

Now you will have some gentle riding through reforested areas and soon come to the lean-to and large horse barn. You might wish to stop for a bit and catch a drink from your bike bottle. Just ahead you have a lengthy climb, punctuated by some diagonal water bars in the trail and then, after some easy trail riding, you will arrive at Truck Trail 1 again (Mile 2.8). (Trail 17 actually goes north and intersects TT 7 but that segment has been closed off — watch for changes as maintenance work is done on the trails.)

Turn right and scoot down the long hill, passing Trail 48 on the right as you start down. This is a great descent, ending with a moderate climb up to Truck Trail 7. Continue straight and just ahead you'll see the left turn for Truck Trail 2 which begins with a steep downhill. After a climb and another climb (Like the previous route, you seem to be either screaming downhill or grunting uphill in granny gears.) you'll come to the intersection with Truck Trail 5 at Mile 3.7. Turn right.

Just ahead on your right through the hemlocks is Lost Pond. Take a little detour in on one of the access trails and check it out. Stark dead trees rise quietly out of the bog — it is quite a lovely spot. If you are in a mood to explore, across Truck Trail 5, if you follow the stream, there is a pretty waterfall down in the woods.

Continuing on TT5, take Trail 23 which jogs off to the left just beyond Lost Pond. This will give you a half-mile of single-track riding over to Truck Trail 4. Turn right and climb up the hill. At the intersection with TT 1, keep climbing up steeply to the right and take the next left on Truck Trail 14. (If you need to shorten the ride, simply take TT1 south to the starting point.)

When you come to the old fire tower site (Mile 5) turn right, pedal past the picnic areas and straight through the parking lot. The trail will be cut up because of the many horse rides starting here so the riding is very technical but at least it is downhill. Bear to the left and soon you will come to Trail 24 which is marked with brown medallions with a horse silhouette. At the intersection with Trail 51, turn right toward Woodland Pond.

You may encounter llama trekkers on the back trails of Baker Forest.

There's a nice little run down to the pond with ledge outcroppings and rocky stretches to test your riding skills. The pond is pretty and a nice place to stop for a snack (Don't expect a concession stand!). Pedal across the dike and take the left fork on to Trail 21.

You'll have a challenging section of puddles, roots, and steep climbs facing you coming out of Woodland Pond. You'll probably notice tire tracks for this is a favorite mountain biking section for local riders. It's easy to see why as the trail levels off and features a great downhill run, past groves of young evergreens, ending with a steep descent to Truck Trail 7.

Turning right on TT7, you're going to gain back a lot of the elevation you just lost, so gear down and tough it out — it is a long steep climb. The ride levels on top at Mile 7 near a shale pit and just ahead, after a quick drop, you'll come to Truck Trail 1. Turn left and you'll see that the long downhill, so enjoyable an hour ago, is now an long uphill on the way out. But it is the last major climb and after that you'll coast past Furman Mills Road at Mile 9.2. The rest of the trip is easy riding on the wide truck trail. At the pavement, turn left and retrace your route back to the car.

Ithaca Area Rides

Texas Hollow Tromp   14 miles
Advanced -- Very steep single-track climbs and descents

Blueberry Patch Ramble   12 miles
Beginner/Intermediate

Virgil Mountain Potpourri   15 miles
Intermediate

Connecticut Hill Loop   11 miles
Intermediate/Advanced

Danby Loop   10 miles
Intermediate

Straits Corners Loop   14 miles
Intermediate -- Mostly dirt roads

Danby Long Loop   15 miles
Intermediate/Advanced

Shindagin Hollow Loop   16 miles
Intermediate/Advanced

Caroline/Hammond Hill Loop   13.5 miles
Intermediate/Advanced

A beaver pond along the Finger Lakes Trail (Danby Long Loop).

Texas Hollow Tromp

14 miles

Advanced — Very steep single-track climbs and descents

After some climbing on a Jeep trail, you will have to negotiate two miles of very difficult hiking trail down to the Texas Hollow Wildlife Refuge. The return route has some lengthy steep climbs on dirt roads and then a long descent back to the start. You will have to carry/push the bike in spots — thus the ride's name.

How To Get There

From Ithaca, take Route 13 southwest toward Elmira to the intersection with Route 224. Follow Route 224 northwest and then turn right on Schuyler County Route 10. In two miles, you will come to Route 228 and see the Finger Lakes Trail coming in from the right. There is ample parking on the shoulder of the road.

The Ride

Take Steam Mill Road and cross Route 228, heading up past States Farm. You are heading out on the Finger Lakes Trail which is marked with white blazes. You'll spot the white vertical dashes on road signs and telephone poles along the dirt road and on trees in the woods.

Just after the equipment building on Steam Mill Road, watch for a foot bridge across the ditch on the right. Gear down and you should be able to pedal across it and up the gravel road that is cut into the bank behind two house trailers. The initial climb is steep but manageable, and soon the roadway gets easier to ride as you intersect a trail frequented by all-terrain vehicles. Continue the long steady climb up the old farm road.

After Mile 1, you will have one last climb up a steep rocky section and then level off and have nearly a mile of easy riding on a grassy tree-lined farm road. At Mile 1.8, the road comes out into a large meadow and the FLT blazes bring you sharply left, then right, past a small pond and a private campground. (Mile 2) Swing right and you will have some pretty scenery ahead as you pedal down the gravel road to the intersection. Turn left at the junction.

Drop down the hill, ignoring the road that pitches off to the right, and climb up through lovely fields toward the solitary grove of trees. You might want to stop for a minute in the shade to catch a drink and look back at the pretty view of Cayuta Lake.

The FLT blazes will guide you down around the bend on Carley Road for a steady descent to the intersection with Steam Mill Road. (Mile 3.2) Get ready for an adventure straight ahead.

The Finger Lakes Trail sign is dead ahead and as soon as you drop down the path and come to a boggy brook with a "balance-on-the-log" crossing, you will get an early taste of the next few miles. You'll have to carry your bike up the far bank and much of the way up the hill. The trail is often muddy and cut up by horses and only when you get on top will you be able to ride. The challenge here is to see just how much of the segment you can ride.

At Mile 3.5, you'll be on top and have a welcome stretch on the saddle and soon come to Newtown Road. Cross it and enter state land. There will be some nice single-track riding along the contours before the trail pitches down quite steeply. Several logs and remnants of a stonewall will have you hopping on and off the bike and shortly, you will intersect an old road. Turn right for a brief level stretch. This trail is not well-marked in spots, nor is it well-groomed, so be ready to plow through some briars.

The trail pitches down to the left through a bramble patch. Looking down through the trees, you can see the valley below. Yes, that's where you're going. At Mile 4.5, there are several "Are you serious?" downhills which will call for more bike carrying. As the

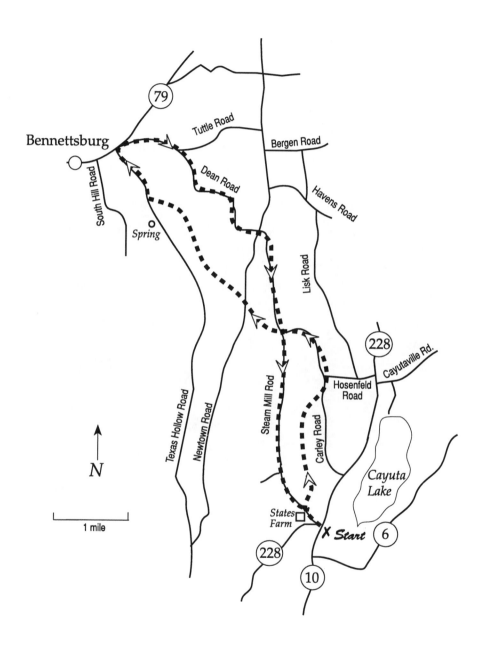

Bennettsburg

79

Tuttle Road

Bergen Road

Dean Road

Havens Road

South Hill Road

Spring

Lisk Road

228

Cayutaville Rd.

Hosenfeld Road

Texas Hollow Road

Newtown Road

Steam Mill Rod

Carley Road

Cayuta Lake

N

1 mile

States Farm

✗ Start

6

228

10

trail descends, there are a lot of chances to ride short stretches. As you get to the bottom, notice how cool it is. Take a moment to listen to the birds.

Off to your left, you can get some glimpses of the boggy pond that marks the wildlife sanctuary as the trail gets better and more rideable. At Mile 5.2, you'll arrive at an opening in the woods and see the dam and outlet from the pond. Pedal down through the outlet stream and ride across the berm, pausing to look at the small marsh. Any herons fishing? At Mile 5.7, you'll come to the Texas Hollow Road. Just think, you could have driven here!

Pausing at the spring on Texas Hollow Road.

Ready for a cool drink? The local watering hole is a year-round spring located less than half a mile south. Turn left and cruise up the shady road — you'll find cold water spewing out of a pipe on the right side of the road. I can attest to its quality and coolness. Fill up the water bottle for you have some serious climbing ahead.

The marsh at Texas Hollow Bird Refuge.

Reverse course and retrace your route back up the Texas Hollow Road for some easy riding. This road, because it is often dusty, is oiled or paved near each dwelling. You'll reach Route 79 at Mile 7.3. Turn right.

After just a short little drop on the shoulder of Route 79, turn right on Tuttle Road and start a major climb. Turn right on Dean Road and cruise by several homes on the level section before starting another climb.

This section of the ride may remind you of mountain biking in Vermont. You're climbing on a dirt road up past small farms and the mountains ahead are covered with hardwoods. There's even a maple syrup operation. See that radio antenna way up ahead? That's where you are heading.

Dean Road turns to a seasonal road and has a mile-long climb with a couple of very steep sections. Just before the top, you'll have some wonderful views off to the west and then, at Mile 10, finally struggle up by the radio tower.

Just as the road levels, you will again meet Newtown Road.

Continue straight ahead and you'll be rewarded with nice views off to the east. Now it's an easy ride home as you swing to the south.

Steam Mill Road is rough gravel but level except for one brief climb at Mile 10.5. Then you'll have a great mile-long descent to the intersection with Carley Road. Continue straight ahead and enjoy a long gradual downhill run back to Route 228 and your car.

Blueberry Patch Ramble

12 miles

Beginner/Intermediate

Single track riding on the Finger Lakes Trail and Interloken National Recreational Trail followed by a return via dirt roads. Sections of the trail are difficult to ride due to damage from horses.

How To Get There

From Ithaca, take Route 79 west through Mecklenburg to Bennettsburg. Turn right by the large barn on to County Route 4 and travel north one mile to Wyckoff Road. Turn right and at the first intersection, turn right and descend a half mile to the parking area in the Finger Lakes National Forest.

From Watkins Glen, take Route 414 to Route 79. Head east through Burdett continuing toward Bennettsburg. County Road 4 will be on the left just before you climb the hill. Turn north by the large barn and travel one mile to Wyckoff Road. At the first intersection, turn right and descend a half mile to the parking area in the Finger Lakes National Forest.

The Ride

From the parking area, follow the Finger Lakes Trail sign toward the shelter. The trail, blazed in white, heads toward the east and the first quarter mile is easy single-track riding on pine needles. After a couple of dry creek crossings, you will dip down to the larger creek (dry in summer) and then start a more difficult climb over rubble-strewn road bed. The climb is steady and as you huff and puff upward, at Mile 1 you will pass the shelter which is set in a little clearing off to the right.

Just up ahead is the junction of the Finger Lakes Trail and the Interloken Trail. Take the Interloken Trail to the right. (This trail is 12 miles in length — you will ride about half it on this loop.)

The Interloken National Recreational Trail is 12 miles long.

The first section of the Interloken Trail (which is marked with orange blazes) is relatively level. It has just enough roots and wet spots to make it technically challenging. Many horseback riders use the trail so you'll encounter many wet spots that are cut up quite badly and difficult to negotiate on bike. At Mile 1.5, pass the Southslope Trail, which pitches down to the left, and follow the more worn Interloken Trail.

After a half-mile more of trail riding, you'll arrive at South

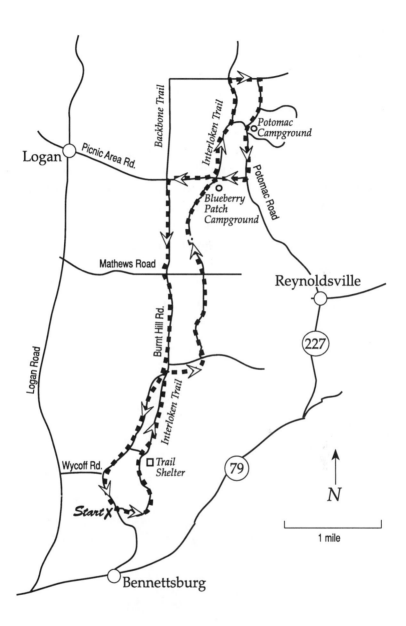

Logan

Picnic Area Rd.

Backbone Trail

Interloken Trail

Potomac Campground

Potomac Road

Blueberry Patch Campground

Mathews Road

Reynoldsville

Burnt Hill Rd.

227

Logan Road

Interloken Trail

Wycoff Rd.

☐ Trail Shelter

79

N

1 mile

Start X

Bennettsburg

Burnt Hill Pond, an impoundment which is typical of the numerous wildlife ponds in the Finger Lakes National Forest. It has been stocked in the past with bass. As you ride along the berm, see if you can spot any of them in the shallow water. (Mile 2.0)

Continue straight ahead on the path which is narrow and flat. A quarter of a mile later, as you meet the gorge trail, bear left on the Interloken Trail and follow the signs to the recreation site. You'll have level riding but may end up thinking unkindly thoughts of horses and their riders as you come upon the cut up trail sections. You will cruise along smoothly for a bit and then, rounding a bend, find a mucky spot deeply-scarred by horses' hoofs. See how many of the tough spots you can ride— it builds character .

After a mile of this on again off again riding, you will arrive at an open space with a wonderful view to the west. (Mile 3.) As you leave the woods, note the tall white plastic pipes sticking up out of the ground. These are experimental tree shelters, developed in Europe, to accelerate the growth of seedlings and protect the young stock from grazing animals.

Admire the great views to the west at Mile 3.

Speaking of grazing, just across the road is part of the Hector Land Use Area, a grazing area for cooperative members who bring their beef and dairy cattle to National Forest pastures from May 15 to October 15. Ride over and enter the gate, closing it behind you. The trail through the pasture may be difficult to pick up in the tall grass. It heads diagonally to the left past the lone tree in the meadow and drops down the contour line to a gate on the far side.

Enter the woods and you will have more of the same — great riding interspersed with cut up areas. Your approach to the Blueberry Patch Recreation Area will be marked by wild blueberries along the trail. As you come to the road (Picnic Area Road), turn right and you will be at the Recreation Area.

Blueberry Patch Campground has nine camp sites and could be a launching point for a number of mountain bike rides. A fee is charged for overnight use, which is on a first-come, first served basis. Between the Forest Service map and a U.S.G.S. topo map (Burdett), it is easy to design a number of loops on trails and back roads from here.

Continue east on the road past the campground and you'll immediately see the Interloken Trail heading off to the left. This well-traveled stretch of trail is relatively level and since it is close to the Backbone Horse Camp, is frequently used by equestrians. Be alert for horses as you head north. At Mile 5.6, when you come to a woods road, turn right and ride the quarter mile to the trailhead parking area at Potomac Road.

Turn right on Potomac Road and cruise down by the Potomac Group Campsite. You will then have a steep downhill run to the intersection with Picnic Area Road at Mile 7.2. Turn right and climb back up to the Blueberry Patch Campground and then descend on the dirt road down to the next intersection. Turn left by the Red House Country Inn on to Burnt Hill Road. The return route, as you can see from the map, is parallel to your route during the first half of the ride.

Burnt Hill Road is level for a half mile and then has a few moderate climbs. Up to your left, you'll see the grazing area that you traversed earlier. Continue straight ahead and you will have some fast riding on the smooth dirt road. Just after Mile 10, swing around the bend by the South Burnt Hill Pond and enjoy some shady riding on the return leg.

Leaving the Finger Lakes Forest, you have a sharp descent to the intersection with Wyckoff Road at Mile 11.5. At the junction, bear left and cruise back down to the shaded parking area. As you put the bike away, you may want to check the ripeness of the fruit on the nearby berry bushes.

Virgil Mountain Potpourri

15 miles

Intermediate

This ride has a mixture of back roads, paved and dirt, along with several miles of the Finger Lakes Trail. When you stir in some hills and great views, you have a mountain biking outing ready to go.

How To Get There

From Ithaca, take Route 13 east to Dryden, then Route 38 south to Harford. Turn left (east) on Route 221 and follow it to Babcock Creek Road.

From Owego, take Route 38 north to Harford Mills, turning right on Route 200. At the intersection of Route 221, head east for 1.3 miles to Babcock Creek Road. Park on the south side of Route 221 on the wide shoulder of the road.

The Ride

Head north on the paved Babcock Creek Road and enjoy some easy pedaling on the quiet smooth road. You are heading up Babcock Hollow and the shady road, following the creek, is a good way to loosen your legs up for the climbs that are up ahead.

As you come to a farm complex at Mile 1.7, turn right on Bleck Road. Just ahead, at Mile 2, a seasonal road climbs steeply off to the right. This will be a tough climb but it is shady and as you ascend, you'll have some heifers for company — they spend the summer up here. At Mile 2.6, climb past the road that goes off to the right and you will note the orange blazes that mark the State Forest. You will be riding in and out of the James B. Kennedy State Forest throughout this ride.

Continue the steep climb and at Mile 3, you finally will level off. Looking ahead, you'll see another road heading off to the right. Take it and let the bike roll down the descending dirt road. Finally, a little downhill!

The Virgil Mountain Loop has many climbs and descents on dirt roads.

Ignore the road coming in from the left at Mile 3.5 and continue downhill, crossing the creek and pedaling through a clearing to the intersection with Fritts Hill Road. (Mile 4.2) Turn left.

Swing down the left fork as you descend and after passing several homes, you will come to pavement. Continue straight, watching for the Quail Hollow Road turn just ahead at Mile 4.9.

Turn left on to the paved Quail Hollow Road which will climb slightly through some pastures. There are homes scattered along the route but the traffic is light. This is easy riding with a couple of climbs and drops.

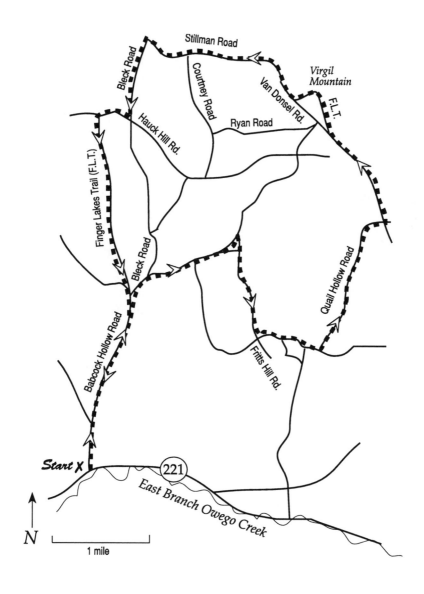

Stillman Road

Bleck Road

Courtney Road

Virgil Mountain

Van Donsel Rd.

F.L.T.

Hauck Hill Rd.

Ryan Road

Finger Lakes Trail (F.L.T.)

Bleck Road

Quail Hollow Road

Babcock Hollow Road

Fritts Hill Rd.

Start X

221

East Branch Owego Creek

N

1 mile

Just after crossing under the power line, you'll pass a lovely home and start climbing as the road reverts to dirt again. At Mile 6.5, you'll come to a four way intersection. Bear left on Valentine Hill Road and immediately start uphill. This is a tough climb but you only have a quarter mile to go before you can level off and catch your breath.

At Mile 7, there will be a dirt road coming in from the right but continue straight ahead. Cross a creek and start up again at Mile 7.3 for another short steep climb. As you arrive at the power line again, bear right and pedal up the service road that parallels the lines.

Although the power lines detract from the scenery, there are some nice views off to the east as you follow the service road. You'll see apricot-colored blazes on rocks that mark the Finger Lakes Trail. Continue to the top and as the road starts to drop, watch for the turn — the FLT heads up to the left. Before you enter the woods, look back for a moment and enjoy the view. Then you will have to push your bike to follow the blazes up into the woods.

As you move up the trail, you'll find it well-worn and easy to ride except for a few downed logs. It is a short climb to the top of Virgil Mountain and the U.S. Coast and Geodetic Survey marker signifying 2132 feet. As local hikers say, it's all downhill from here — well, almost.

The FLT drops down to Van Donsel Road at Mile 8.3. When you get there, turn right and cruise down the hill. Off to your right, over the lip of the hill, is the Greek Peak ski area. Climb back up into State Forest along Van Donsel Road through some stately conifers lining both sides of the road.

At Mile 9, there is a gated access road heading up to the right as you cruise down around the corner. At the bottom, there's another access road off to the right. Just ahead is perhaps the steepest climb so far. As you huff and puff to the top, note the stately maples lining the road and the new ski chalet stuck in the meadow to your right. You will see in a moment why it was placed there.

At the intersection at Mile 10.1, go straight, descending down past a number of houses. As you see the views off to the north, you can understand why so many new homes, such as the chalet, have

The sign posted at the top of Virgil Mountain.

sprung up here. Cruise down on pavement but don't get carried away, you'll soon turn left soon. Up ahead you can see the Village of Virgil as you get ready to turn left on to Bleck Road.

After a short climb on pavement up Bleck Road, you'll start down again and the road goes back to dirt on a nice downhill. At Mile 11, at the four-way intersection, turn right. Drop down and after crossing a creek, climb up to the rise. Voila`! You have been rewarded with a wonderful view to the west. Don't descend on the road; turn on to the Finger Lakes Trail which is up to your left.

The FLT, again blazed in apricot, is an old Jeep trail, and has a couple of pretty good climbs before you get a wonderful downhill.

Having just seen that great view to the west, you are tantalized, as you climb, by glimpses through the foliage of valleys and barns and clouds, and mostly trees.

Follow the trail downhill as the road gets more narrow and at Mile 12.5, you will intersect the main east-west Finger Lakes Trail, blazed in white. Continue straight ahead on the right-of-way and you will come to a clearing. Follow the rocky farm road down through hay fields and after a last bumpy descent, you'll arrive again at the intersection with Babcock Hollow Road at Mile 13. Continue straight ahead. The return on pavement is an easy cool-down on the wide paved road to your car back on Route 221.

Connecticut Hill Loop

11 miles

Intermediate/Advanced

Connecticut Hill, at 2,095 feet, is one of the highest point in the eastern Finger Lake region. Geologists go into overdrive when they describe it, saying, in the the words of one, "... that it shows how the highest elevations of the peneplain upland surface appear where the rock strata are downbent, have synclinal structure."

For the mountain biker, this translates into "difficult climbs and challenging descents." After starting out easily, this loop climbs up to the top of the Connecticut Hill plateau. It ends with a long steep descent and a level cool down segment.

Connecticut Hill is a state wildlife management area so expect to see deer, turkeys, or grouse. Do not ride in this area during hunting season.

Bring a map and compass for there are a number of trails and roads in this area that you may wish to explore. The USGS maps for this area are Mecklenburg-Alpine. You should bring food and water with you.

How To Get There
From Ithaca, take Route 13 southwest for 13 miles. Watch for the D.E.C. sign on the right just after you pass Sebring Road.

From the Route 17 in the Elmira area, take Route 13 north for 12 miles to the junction with Route 224. Continue on Route 13 toward Ithaca for another 5 miles. Once you pass the Connecticut

Hill Road, the turn on to Carter Creek Road will be on your left just after a white barn.

Take Carter Creek road. After a half mile, just after you pass by a chalet home on the left, you'll come to a turn-out which has room for parking.

The Ride

From the parking site, continue up Carter Creek Road which will be marked as a "Seasonal-Limited Use" road. The initial stretch of riding is level through fields of goldenrod and burdocks. Note the shale outcroppings on both sides. In the first half mile, you'll cross a one-lane bridge over Carter Creek and start gently uphill and ride on to D.E.C. land. Look off to the right as you climb and see if you can spot the old dam site through the trees.

After pedaling up to the first intersection, continue straight ahead and pitch down the curved little run and climb up the other side. At Mile 1.2, you'll arrive at another intersection with a road climbing off to the left. Take a good look — that's the type of climb that will be ahead later on — for now, continue straight ahead on the flatter Carter Creek Road.

You're circling the plateau at this point as you can tell by the steep hills to your left. You'll see some open fields with gnarled apple trees remaining from the past farming that once marked this area. At Mile 2, swing down and cross the creek one last time and then start a steep climb up through lovely stands of pine. At Mile 2.4, the climb ends and just ahead is an intersection. Turn left and get ready for another quarter-mile climb.

Pause on top to catch your breath and then you can enjoy a wonderful downhill run. There well may be some large puddles at the bottom so either blast through or miss them as is your wont. You will come to a three-way intersection at Mile 3.5.

The road off to the right heads toward Trumbell Corners. Take a short ride down it for a pretty pastoral view of a beef farm and off in the distance, the Ithaca area. This is a good spot to relax and snack for there's another major climb facing you.

Retrace your route back to the intersection and take the wide

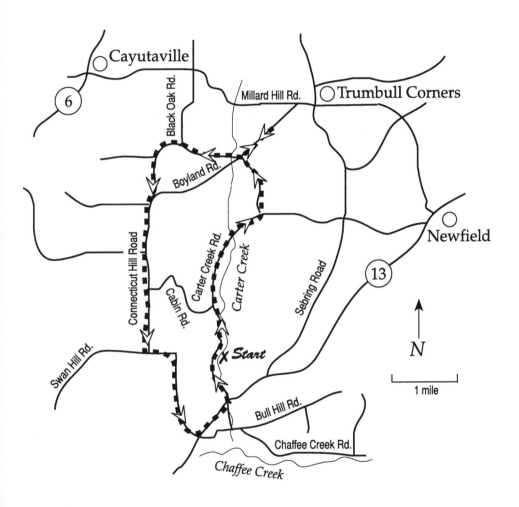

road that bears right and passes by a lovely pond before starting uphill. This is a beauty of a climb, over a half mile in length with no letup. At Mile 4.8, a road goes off to the left as the main road climbs to the right. Take the narrow road to the left that is marked "Seasonal Use Highway — No Maintenance Dec 1 — April 1."

After just a short uphill, the road now levels off, finally, and you can look forward to some easy riding up here on top. As you cruise along, you'll pass several roads that pitch down off the plateau to the right toward Cayuta Lake. Continue straight ahead. (There are several trails intersecting this stretch, including the Finger Lakes Trail, that offer some single-track riding if you are so inclined.)

At Mile 6, when you come to an intersection with the Boyland Hill Road coming in from the right, why not dismount and take a moment to explore the old graveyard?

Continuing straight ahead, pass by a road heading off to the right and soon you'll see a mile-long straight stretch ahead. With just a few rough spots and mud, this will be a welcome downhill run. Ignore the road pitching down to the right at Mile 6.5 and start a long straight descent which will end with a steep little drop down to the "T" intersection at Mile 8. Turn left.

After an initial climb, you're going to be in for the downhill of your life. This is Connecticut Hill Road, a steep winding unimproved road which is rough and rutted and may well have little streams running down it. Use the brakes judiciously and keep your legs flexed to absorb the bumps. As you depart the state land, you will note that the property on both sides is now posted. The last segment of the downhill is the best — a steep twisting drop down to the brook at Mile 9.5. If your heart is not pounding from excitement, you can hear the cars on Route 13 up ahead.

Turn left once you come to the main highway and pedal back up the wide bike lane about a half mile up to Carter Creek Road. Turn left and cruise the last half mile back to your car.

Danby Loop

10 miles

Intermediate

This is a moderately difficult ride through parts of the Danby State Forest with several steep climbs on back dirt roads. After starting with a half-mile steep climb, you will ride on a rolling Jeep trail with several rutted, technical downhills. Then, after a long descent, you will gain back 600' in elevation and end with a screaming downhill to the parking area.

Bring a map and compass for there are a number of trails and roads in this area that you may wish to explore including the Finger Lakes Trail. The USGS map for this area is Willseyville.

How To Get There

From Ithaca, take Route 96B up past Ithaca College about 6 miles to Danby. Turn right on the Michigan Hollow Road and travel south for 2.4 miles. The parking area is on the left where an unmarked dirt road heads uphill. There are trail markers for the Finger Lakes Trail as well.

From Spencer, take Route 34/96 north to North Spencer. Just past a church school, turn right on Michigan Hollow Road. You will pass Signor Hill Road on the right at about two miles and at four miles, come to another dirt road that climbs off to the right. This is the parking site.

The Ride

Your first climb is a steep half mile so you may want to warm your legs up a bit on the Michigan Hollow Road before setting out.

Get into a granny gear and climb up the dirt road that links Michigan Hollow Road with Irish Hill Road. Note how the water has cut little stair-steps out of the ledge on your right as you grunt your way to the top. Take heart, you'll be coasting down this hill at the ride's end. After one last steep section, you'll arrive at Irish Hill Road. Turn left and head down the wide dirt road.

Cruise down a short downhill and climb to the intersection of Hill Road and Curtis Road at Mile 1. Turn right on to Curtis, which is a seasonal road, and you'll pedal past a gravel pit and sawmill. After riding by an upland meadow, you will come to the State Forest and enjoy a slightly downhill ride on the rutted seasonal road. This is great mountain bike riding territory.

At Mile 2, you will cross the Finger Lakes Trail and have a half-mile downhill which is steep and which may have a few washed out sections. After you traverse a small stream at Mile 2.5, you will have another mile of easy riding as Curtis Road heads down to Fisher Settlement Road. Turn right at the junction.

Fisher Settlement Road is wide and smooth and generally downhill. Just after Mile 4, you will descend by the Lions Children's Camp and then, after a short climb, hit paved road for the first time on the ride. Now there will be a fast steady downhill of about a mile. As you pass the new log home near the bottom of the long hill, slow down for a turn to the right on to Signor Hill Road.

This is a pretty country road. You will pass a dilapidated barn and climb up past an old farmhouse on smooth dirt. Just after Mile 6, State Forest land begins again. You will see Signor Hill Road swinging left (down to Michigan Hollow Road) but you should continue straight up the unmarked dirt road.

As you start up through the pines on a steep climb, notice the lovely smell from the conifers. Hang in there, the climb is steady for nearly a half mile and there are several rutted spots — but that's what mountain bikes are built for. At the top, pause for a moment and note the brook far down in the gorge — and as your pulse slows,

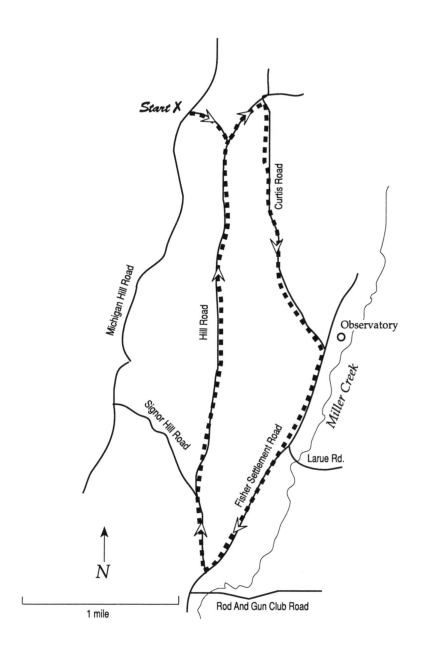

you'll likely hear a few chickadees in the hemlocks lining the bank.

After a short respite, you'll climb again in a series of ascents, all less steep than the first climb. At Mile 8, the route levels off for a half mile of easy riding. Watch for old apple trees and stonewall remnants that mark the old farmsteads along the way. You also may notice, as we do too often on back roads, indiscriminate dumping of trash and debris.

The last mile on this road is level to slightly uphill but the climbs are easier when you remember the nice descent to the parking area at the end. At Mile 9, you will again pass the Finger Lakes Trail and a half mile later, exit the forest road. Continue straight ahead down a little grade past several homes and watch for the left turn on to the seasonal road which comes up in less than a quarter mile.

The last downhill is a screamer. Keep your legs flexed and enjoy the quick trip back down to the car.

Straits Corners Loop

14 miles

Intermediate — Mostly dirt roads

This is a "plain vanilla" ride through the old farm country of Tioga County with lots of varied riding on back dirt roads. Most of the roads have "Hill" in their name so get ready for some climbing.

How To Get There

From Ithaca, take Route 96 south to Spencer, then east to West Candor. Turn right on Straits Corners Road and wind your way south for a little over five miles to the Straits Corners Baptist Church. There is parking on the shoulder of the road.

From Route 17 in Owego, take Route 96 north to Candor and continue west on Route 96 for three miles, watching for the Straits Corners Road on the left. Follow the road south to the church.

The Ride

From the church, head north on pavement and immediately turn left on to Southwick Hill Road. As you pedal past a small farm, you will see a "Seasonal Use Road" sign — always an invitation to interesting mountain biking. Take it.

The route starts with a pretty good climb on rough dirt for about a quarter of a mile. There are old pastures on each side and as you crest the hill, pull off to the left to catch your breath and admire the view. The landowner reports that several wild turkeys nest each spring in the middle of that hayfield.

The ride begins and ends at the church.

The road continues with a series of climbs and descents as you travel through old pasture land. That's Chambers Creek off to your left. If you're sharp-eyed, you may spot an old outhouse nested in the woods to the left as you pedal over the culvert at Mile 1.0.

Just ahead on the right, there's a pretty beaver pond but respect the "Land Posted" signs. The riding through here is easy with a few bony spots where the road has washed out. After a short climb at Mile 2, the road levels and you'll have some pretty views off to the left. Cruise for a half mile and you'll be at the intersection of Chapel and Shumaker roads. Continue straight ahead.

Shumaker Road is slightly downhill and has a series of homes along it — watch out for dogs as you coast by. At the bottom of the easy descent at Mile 3.0, turn left on to Cass Road (by the house with the butterflies on it) and pedal along on rough pavement. You have a taste of the route now — a typical rural New York setting of forest, pasture, occasional rural homes and trailers, and dairy farms.

The route climbs past a dairy farm and past a small impound-

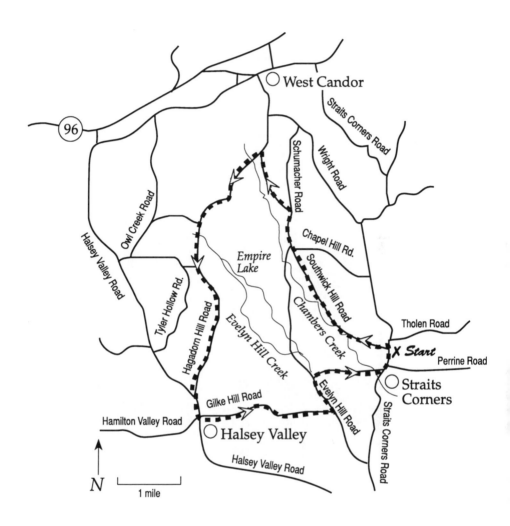

ment with the obligatory flock of Canada geese. As Cass Road starts downhill, turn left on Cooper and get ready to climb. There is a pretty serious climb at Mile 4.1 for a half mile up past a series of homes. As you get to the top, roll right past the dirt road that goes straight ahead at Mile 5.0 (it is a dead end) and sweep down around the bend to the right on the wider dirt road. At the end of the drop, Shaw Road goes off to the right. Continue on Hagadorn Hill Road.

There's a pretty beaver pond just before Mile 2.0.

After a brief uphill, notice the old farmhouse on the right surrounded by lilac trees. This is typical of the farmsteads in this area and if you ride the route in late May, the scenery and the smells are wonderful. Off to the right, the views are striking and you can see several tree farms with their rows of evergreens marching up the hillside. Hagadorn is a nice rolling dirt road and finishes with a long downhill of over a mile ending at Halsey Valley Road.

The area is dotted with old farm buildings.

Be careful turning left on Halsey Valley — you only have a few hundred yards to ride and there is a narrow dirt shoulder to use. Swing left on Gilkie Hill Road and get ready to gain back some of the elevation you just lost on that wonderful downhill. As you labor up the loose gravel road, take heart that the ride ends with a wonderful downhill run. At Mile 10, you'll be on top and can enjoy some nice backcountry riding. Another abandoned farmhouse lies just ahead and then, after a mile, the road comes to the Gilkie Hill Deer Farm. Note the deer pens — perhaps if you are sharp-eyed, you may spot some of the small red deer. (Fallow deer raising is a popular business in several parts of Central New York.)

Continue down the steep drop and shortly you'll arrive at the intersection with Eveline Hill Road (Mile 11.5). Turn left. Cruise for about a half mile and as you pass an old barn, you'll note an "Old McDonald's" farm down to the right with dozens of pieces of rusted machinery in the fields. Take the unmarked dirt road that pitches down to the right and runs through the farmstead. Start the steady climb up from the farm and as you level off, you will enter a wooded area and be treated to some mud and rough road as well as a winding, steep downhill. This challenging descent is a fitting end to the ride.

Pedal out to the pavement (Mile 13.5) and turn left, enjoying the smooth and level half-mile stretch back to the church.

Danby Long Loop

15 miles

Intermediate/Advanced

This is a challenging ride with some steep climbs on back dirt roads and two sections of the Finger Lakes Trail. You start with a technical ride on the Finger Lakes Trail and then have a series of steep downhills and long climbs on smooth dirt roads. The last several miles are on the Finger Lakes Trail and have several "push your bike" uphills. The route ends with a screaming downhill to the parking area. Plan three hours or so for this outing — it's worth it.

How To Get There

From Ithaca, take Route 96B up past Ithaca College about 6 miles to Danby. Turn right on the Michigan Hollow Road and travel south for 2.4 miles. The parking area is on the left where an unmarked dirt road heads uphill. There are trail markers for the Finger Lakes Trail as well.

From Spencer, take Route 34/96 north to North Spencer. Right past a church school, turn right on Michigan Hollow Road. You will pass Signor Hill Road on the right at about two miles and at four miles, come to another dirt road that climbs off to the right. This is the parking site.

The Ride

From the parking spot, ride north less than a hundred years and look for the well-marked Finger Lakes Trail going west. Just as you pitch down from the road, you will come to a two-plank crossing of Michigan Creek. (How's your balance? I recommend walking the bike.) Follow the white blazes straight ahead and you will have some easy riding, with just a few logs to hop over, on an abandoned wagon road which heads west.

The well-marked Finger Lakes Trail is great for mountain biking.

Before long, you will come to a challenging climb up a rocky stream bed. The trail gets more rutted and eroded as you proceed and there are a series of climbs that are steep and technical. The trail comes out on Bald Hill Road at Mile 1.6. Now you will get to lose all the elevation, and then some, that you just gained. Turn left.

Bald Hill Road goes downhill steeply on dirt, with a short stretch of pavement. As you steam down at Mile 2, bear left on to the dirt road marked "Seasonal Road." This is still Bald Hill. Keep your speed up for there is a climb ahead.

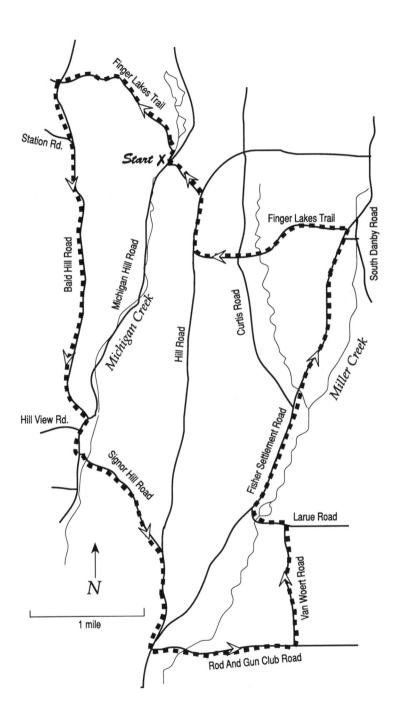

Finger Lakes Trail

Station Rd.

Start X

Finger Lakes Trail

South Danby Road

Bald Hill Road

Michigan Hill Road

Michigan Creek

Hill Road

Curtis Road

Miller Creek

Fisher Settlement Road

Hill View Rd.

Signor Hill Road

Larue Road

Van Woert Road

N

1 mile

Rod And Gun Club Road

The climb is steep but less than a quarter mile in length. About half way up you'll spot a cemetery on the right. As you level off in the Danby State Forest, you will have some lovely back dirt road riding to Mile 4. The route then starts a mile-long descent ending with a level stretch and a final steep drop lined with wild flowers down to the paved Michigan Hollow Road. (Mile 5.1)

Turn right and enjoy a brief downhill cruise on smooth pavement. Pass by the road going off to the right and continue straight ahead, looking for Signor Hill Road on the left.

Signor Hill is steep, a real gut-buster — there's no better way to say it. Take your time and grunt up the 200 feet in elevation to the top at Mile 6. Then you will have smooth riding on dirt and pass a pretty beaver pond just after Mile 6.6. Bear right and continue cruising on a gentle downhill run, coming out on the Fisher Settlement Road at Mile 7.2. Bear right.

After just a brief stint on pavement, turn left on Hart Road (also called Rod & Gun Club Road.) Pedal up by the club on the flat road. Then you will start a series of climbs that are the most prolonged of any in this book — a 400 foot rise in elevation in about three-quarters of a mile. The first two climbs are manageable but the third one is really steep — if you are like me, you'll want to get off and push just to use other leg muscle groups. Finally, as you grunt to the top, what do you see but a stop sign. Sick humor after that climb.

Continue straight ahead and enjoy a short little downhill on pavement. Turn left on the dirt Van Woert Road. Pedal up past some rural homes and in less than a mile you will come to a dead end. Continue ahead on the right-of-way on a single track trail that drops steadily. It will be rutted and cut up by horses and give you some interesting riding. At Mile 9.8, you will outlet on Larue Road. Turn left and drop downhill by the Lions Club camp and climb briefly up to Fisher Settlement Road. Turn right.

Fisher Settlement Road is wide and easy riding for several miles with a couple of good descents and climbs. The first climb is just after you pass the unmarked Curtis Road which comes in from the left at Mile 11.2. You will pass the "Danby Pirates Club" at Mile 12.5, and shortly afterwards, see the familiar Finger Lakes Trail signs on both sides of the road. Turn left and climb up the trail.

Erosion has exposed many rocks and roots on this section of trail.

The first stretch is a "push your bike" uphill through a plantation of evergreens. The trail is rutted and much more single track than the first section on this ride. After a long climb, you will start downhill at once through hardwoods. This descent has many turns and roots to maneuver over — but it is quite rideable. The trail is well marked with white blazes.

Right after the crossing of a tributary of Miller Creek, you'll be faced with a "no way, Jose!" climb. All but the most hardy will push up this one, it's straight up. After a short level stretch, you will come out on Curtis Road. (Mile 14) This has been so much fun, we'll continue straight ahead on the Finger Lakes Trail.

The next section of trail is more heavily used and is a veritable highway compared to what you just finished. After some nice level riding, the route drops through a washed-out section, coming to a lovely small beaver pond. Continue to follow the white blazes up the far side of the pond and you will have a fairly steep climb to where you intersect Hill Road.

Turn right and after a half-mile downhill, with one brief climb, you will exit the forest road. Continue straight ahead down a little grade past several homes and watch for the left turn on to the seasonal road which comes up in less than a quarter mile.

The last downhill is a screamer. Keep your legs flexed and enjoy the quick trip back down to the car.

Shindagin Hollow Loop

16 miles

Intermediate/Advanced

This is a long loop through the Shindagin Hollow State Forest on hilly back roads with some single-track riding on the Finger Lakes Trail. You will start on dirt roads and then traverse three miles of challenging trail riding. After a long stretch of back road riding, you will finish with a long fast descent on pavement.

How To Get There

From Ithaca, take Route 79 for five miles to Route 330. Continue five miles until you come to Old Seventysix Road at Guide Board Corners.

From the east, take Route 79 to Slaterville Springs. Take Old Seventysix Road south to the hamlet of Guide Board Corners.

You can park on the northern shoulder of the Seventysix Road.

The Ride

Chestnut Road, a seasonal use road, climbs south out of Guide Board Corners. You'll have an initial climb with pastures on both sides and then the road levels as you look down at Central Chapel Road off to the right. Downey Road, another seasonal road, heads off to the left but you want to continue straight ahead on the paved road, dropping down to the paved Central Chapel Road at Mile 1.0. Bear left, continuing south on the wide paved road and at the fork ahead, take another left on to Shindagin Hollow Road, which is paved for a short distance.

The road transitions to dirt as you enter the State Forest. Cruise down the hill and at Mile 2.5, just as you start a pretty good downgrade, watch ahead for a Jeep trail bearing off to the right. That's your turn. If you're sharp-eyed, you can spot a small grave site, marked with wooden rails, up to the right. The graves are from the 1830-1860 era, a time when this area was farmed.

The Finger Lakes Trail has plenty of "push your bike" sections.

The Jeep trail is a steady climb but easily ridden. You're likely to see plenty of tire tracks — this section is a favorite with Ithaca-area cyclists. Stay on the main trail which will swing right. At Mile 3.5, you will see the white blazes of the Finger Lakes Trail on the right, and also dropping down the hill to the left. Turn left, descending, noting the old foundation remnants on the right. The trail turns right and follows the contours of the hill, climbing again in spots. This is challenging but interesting mountain bike riding. Looking down to the left, you can see the ravine that forms the Shindagin Hollow. You are going to be losing that much elevation so check your brakes and get ready for some interesting downhill.

The main drop, when it comes, starts nicely across the contours and then goes sharply downhill. Get your weight way back over the

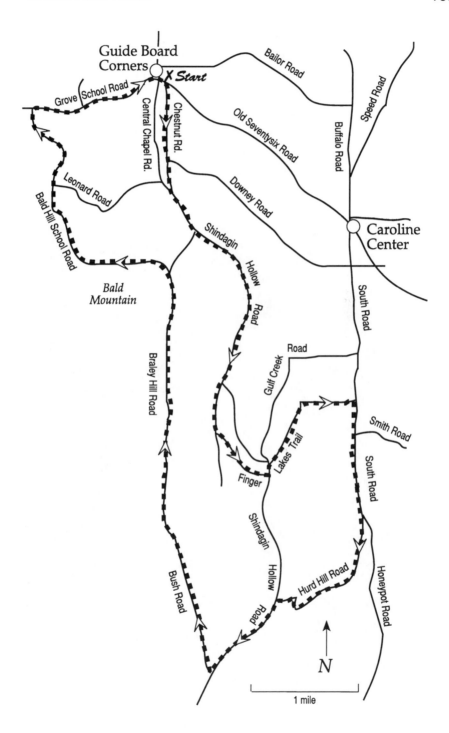

rear wheels and keep your speed under control. After a brief respite, you have a last short descent which ends with some steps. You should negotiate this last stretch on foot. When you come out on Shindagin Hollow Road, turn left. (Mile 4.2)

Just up the road on the right, the trail is well-marked and crosses the Shindagin Hollow Creek on a new footbridge. The trail picks up an old road and climbs steeply, one of the "push your bike" variety. Catch your breath and you can probably ride most of the sections, which continue uphill.

A footbridge over Shindagin Hollow Creek tests your balance.

About Mile 4.8, the trail dips down, jogging left and then right and you'll pass a lean-to set in the hemlocks. There's a steep drop-off to the ravine on your left — this is an impressive sight during the spring runoff.

Follow the gorge for a stretch and then the white blazes take you due east, climbing steadily, for a half-mile until you come out on the paved South Road. Turn right and get ready to enjoy a mile of paved descent. Now you can cool off and chase away any horseflies.

Cruise down past the youth detention center and as you descend, watch for the right turn on to Hurd Hill Road, another seasonal use highway. (Mile 6.3) Hurd Hill Road drops down gently at first through a shaded area with overhanging trees and then starts down a bit more steeply. As you continue, the road condition deteriorates and has some washed out sections, but at least it is all downhill. After a sweeping hairpin turn, you will come out on the Shindagin Hollow Road for the third time. Bear left.

You will now have a half mile of easy riding on the smooth dirt road past several rural homes. As you come to the pavement, turn right on to Bush Road. (Mile 8.5)

Pedal north past several homes and you will re-enter the State Forest in less than half a mile. This is easy riding paralleling a dry (in the summer) creek bed. Approaching Mile 10, there is a slight climb up past several homes and as you level off, a lovely plantation of pines on your left.

After a nice little dip and climb at Mile 10.5, you will come again to the Finger Lakes Trail. (The trail to the right intersects the segment you just rode down to Shindagin Hollow.) Continue straight ahead on the dirt road which continues on with a series of climbs until you come to the unmarked Bald Hill School Road which goes up to the left at Mile 12.2. Turn left.

At this point in the ride, this will be a difficult climb up past some meadows with views off to the right. As you level off, you'll cruise into an old maple grove as you get ready to ride down a winding downhill. This is another shaded, hard-surfaced dirt road just perfect for mountain biking. (There are a number of Bald Hill Roads in New York, reminders of the last century when cattle and sheep grazed these hills. It is sometimes hard to picture since most of the forest has grown back.)

There is a good downhill run from Mile 13 to Mile 14 and you will pass Leonard Road (unmarked) which pitches down to the right. Continuing, you will pedal up to a stretch of new pavement and start to see several new homes. (Check out the innovative home on the right as you descend to the intersection with Grove School Road.) Turn right on to Grove School Road and get ready for a fast, curved downhill run on pavement back to the start — a great end to a great ride.

Caroline/Hammond Hill Loop

13.5 miles

Intermediate/Advanced

This is a challenging ride with plenty of climbing on back dirt roads, moto-cross trails and a section of the Finger Lakes Trail. You will start with a mile warm-up on pavement and then climb on a seasonal use road up to a lovely pond. You now have a long section of single-track riding on moto-cross trails followed by a challenging section of the Finger Lakes Trail. The return is on back roads and jeep trails, with some muddy sections, followed by a long downhill back to Caroline. The last two miles are on level pavement. The USGS map for this area is Dryden.

How To Get There
From Ithaca, take Route 79 to Caroline. Just before the Tompkins/Tioga County line there is a snowplow turnaround area on the north side of the road which has ample room for parking.

The Ride
From the parking spot, pedal east on the shoulder of Route 79, crossing the West Branch of Owego Creek and turning left on to Robinson Hollow Road. Cruise along past some mobile homes and houses and at Mile 1.4, you'll see a sign saying "Narrow Bridge." Turn left on to the unmarked seasonal road and you will have some shaded level riding along the brook. As you start an easy climb into state land, note the large boulder on the left and the ledge waterfall.

At Mile 1.9, get ready for a steady climb. At Mile 2.3, the road gets steeper and is rocky and rough in spots. You'll notice a trail going off to the left along the brook and may see some Boy Scouts camped out.

Just as you level off from the long climb, there's a road to the left and a parking area for a little pond. (This is locally called "Tri-County Pond" because Tioga, Cortland, and Tompkins counties meet here.) Turn left and coast down to the pond.

There is a nice bathing area on the far side if you wish to cool off. When you are ready to continue, pedal up the trail that heads west from the berm of the impoundment and follow it up through pines and stretches of blueberries. Interesting riding lies ahead.

A single-track section on the Caroline/Hammond Hill Loop.

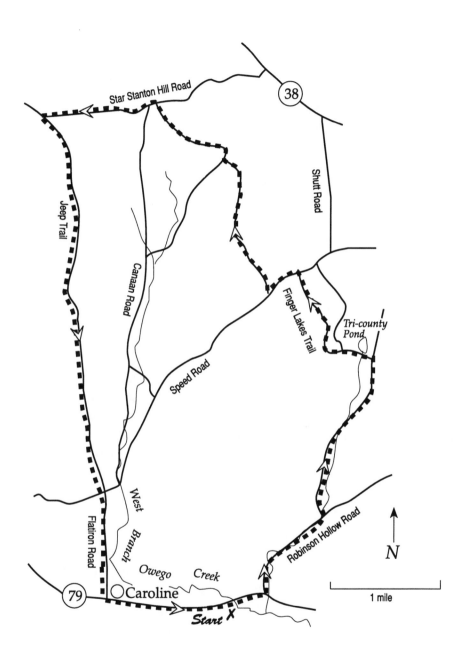

First of all, you'll come down a nice descent which ends in a marshy area where you'll probably have to carry the bike. Pick the driest path and slog through. Climb up the next rise and you will come to a logged-off area. Moto-cross riders have a major trail through here so press on straight ahead and at the west end of the clearing, you'll find a well-worn single-track that heads off to your right toward an old weathered shack. Follow the dirt bike trail north and into the woods. This will be a real tricky section of riding due to the deep gullies cut by the dirt bikes.

As you come out of the woods on single-track, bear right and follow the bike trail down across a small wet section. As you begin to climb, turn left and the trail reverts to an old logging road which winds its way down some technical loose rock riding down to the paved Speed Road. (Mile 4.2) Turn left.

Cruise down the hill on pavement past a dilapidated farm and look for a parking area on the right which will be your turn. As you turn right, you'll see the "No Motorized Vehicles" sign and white blazes that mark the Finger Lakes Trail. Head up the trail and follow the blazes up the hill on a winding climb which follows an old jeep trail. There are several sections that are quite steep but most can be ridden in a granny gear. As you get on top just after Mile 5, the riding is easier. The trail is well-worn for many dirt bike riders use this stretch, even though they are prohibited.

The trail follows the contour lines along the top of the ridge and at Mile 5.7, you'll see a posted trail go off to the right. Peek your head through the bushes and you will see large micro-wave towers and a control building.

Continuing northward, the trail now is more a hiking trail since the moto-cross folks usually turn off at the towers. You'll have some interesting riding ending with a very steep downhill. Be alert at the bottom — you will be leaving the white blazed trail.

At the bottom of the steep drop, where the arrows tell you to swing right to follow the FLT, go straight ahead on another moto-cross trail and follow it downhill. After a wild little drop and climb across a wet spot, you will be at the parking area at the end of a dirt road called Red Man Run.

Pausing to admire the view.

Turn right and pedal up the Jeep trail to a shale pit, swinging to the left and climbing up the bank. The trail now has some great riding, albeit muddy at times, with several stretches of single-track. After navigating a few tricky wet spots, climb up to a four-way intersection — all dirt — all unmarked. By now, your bike and your legs are probably pretty muddy and you should expect to get speckled with mud from your tires on the downhill just ahead.

As you come out to the "T" intersection, turn left and climb up the short hill on the unsigned Star Stanton Road. (Mile 6.8) You then will have a long run downhill that starts on very rough road and then smooths out, after you pass a farm on the right, into a long cooling downhill run. This will chase the deerflies away.

Turn sharp left on to Hammond Hill Road. (Ignore the road signs if they appear confusing, several were twisted the wrong way when I rode this route.) This is a tough climb this late in the ride but it is short and soon you will be on dirt. At Mile 8.4, you'll pass a summer camp on the right and then the jeep trail starts up, easy at first and then quite steeply. You'll have to push the bike at times.

About Mile 9, you're on top and if there's any breeze, you'll feel it. You will have some major puddles to negotiate and will find that the trail goes off to higher ground on the right side for a stretch. Avoid blasting through the puddles, they are axle-deep and you've still got a lot of riding ahead. This is mountain bike fun — trying to keep upright and dry.

Once the trail starts down, it is a long steady drop. You'll pick up more mud thrown off by the spinning tires. The last mile is smooth and fast and at Mile 11.3, you will come to the intersection with Speed Road. Continue straight ahead on the level Flatiron Road and you will come to Route 79 in another mile.

Carefully cross the highway, turn left, and pedal on the wide shoulder back through Caroline. There are several historic markers along the way and it is an easy cool-down jaunt back to the parking area. Wash that grimy bike when you get it back home.

Acorn Publishing/Vitesse Press Books

Cycling Along The Canals of New York by Louis Rossi $15.95
A guide to 500 miles of bicycle riding along the Erie Canal.

Cycling Health and Physiology by Ed Burke, Ph.D. $17.95
Using sports science to improve your riding and racing. New edition.

Bicycle Road Racing by Edward Borysewicz $24.95
A complete road-racing program by former National Coach Eddie B.

Road Racing: Technique & Training by Bernard Hinault $17.95
Racing and training tips from a five-time Tour de France winner.

Massage For Cyclists by Roger Pozeznik $14.95
Clear advice and excellent photos of massage sequences. 2nd Printing.

Mountain Biking For Women by Robin Stuart & Cathy Jensen $15.00
Woman to woman advice and instruction from two experienced cyclists.

Central New York Mountain Biking by Dick Mansfield $12.95
Thirty of the best back road and trail rides in upstate New York.

Vermont Mountain Biking by Dick Mansfield $10.95
Twenty-four rides in southern Vermont.

Fit and Pregnant by Joan Butler $16.00
Advice from a nurse-midwife who is an athlete and mother. Fourth printing.

Runner's Guide To Cross Country Skiing by Dick Mansfield $10.95
Still the best source for runners looking for a winter alternative.

Canoe Racing by Peter Heed $14.95
The "bible" of flat water canoe racing. Third printing.

We encourage you to buy our books at a bookstore or off our web site. When ordering directly from Vitesse, prepayment or a credit card number and expiration date is required. Include the book price plus handling ($2.50 for the first book, $1.00 for each additional book) and 5% sales tax for Maryland addresses.

Telephone 301-772-5915   Fax 301-772-5921
VITESSE PRESS, 4431 Lehigh Road, #288, College Park, MD 20740

Email: dickmfield@aol.com   Web site: www.acornpub.com